Sexuality

ISSUES
(formerly Issues for the Nineties)

Volume 23

Editor

Craig Donnellan

First published by Independence
PO Box 295
Cambridge CB1 3XP
England

British Library Cataloguing in Publication Data
Sexuality – (Issues Series)
I. Donnellan, Craig II. Series
306.7'66

ISBN 1 86168 179 8

Printed in Great Britain
The Burlington Press
Cambridge

Typeset by
Claire Boyd

Cover
The illustration on the front cover is by
Pumpkin House.

CONTENTS

Chapter One: Addressing Sexuality

Homosexual or gay?	1
Homosexuality is . . .	3
Christianity and homosexuality	5
Straights and gays take to same lifestyle	6
Questions	7
Coming out	9
Sex education	10
Calling for honesty in education	12
Homosexuality	15
Prejudice and discrimination	16
Prejudice against gay men	17
Background to homophobia	18
Fury over gay study	20
Homosexuality and the Church	21
Lesbians, gay men, bisexuals and mental health	22
Identity and sexuality	24
What is the gay gene?	26
Press for Change	27

Chapter Two: The Legal Aspects

Age of consent	29
New battle for gay couples' rights	30
Section 28	31
Gay job protection soon	32
Discrimination against lesbian and gay employees	33
Be biased in favour of gays judges are told	36
Gay partners will get crime payouts	37
Gay marriages	38
Laws relating to young LGBs	39
Now let's have real equality for lesbians and gay men	40
Transsexuals seek marriage rights	40
Additional resources	41
Index	42
Web site information	43
Acknowledgements	44

Introduction

Sexuality is the twenty-third volume in the **Issues** series. The aim of this series is to offer up-to-date information about important issues in our world.

Sexuality examines the issues of homosexuality in society, homophobia and the legal aspects of being homosexual.

The information comes from a wide variety of sources and includes:
Government reports and statistics
Newspaper reports and features
Magazine articles and surveys
Literature from lobby groups
and charitable organisations.

It is hoped that, as you read about the many aspects of the issues explored in this book, you will critically evaluate the information presented. It is important that you decide whether you are being presented with facts or opinions. Does the writer give a biased or an unbiased report? If an opinion is being expressed, do you agree with the writer?

Sexuality offers a useful starting-point for those who need convenient access to information about the many issues involved. However, it is only a starting-point. At the back of the book is a list of organisations which you may want to contact for further information.

*****

Homosexual or gay?

Defining homosexuality

Why are people called homosexual or gay, and what does it mean?

The terms heterosexual and homosexual are rarely used in everyday speech. More often people use slang words or terms which are abusive. Throughout the last century the terms used to describe gay people, and that gay people used to describe themselves, have changed. These changes are important in telling us a lot about how lesbian and gay people lived their lives and felt about themselves as well as social reactions to them. What about the terms 'straight', 'gay' and 'lesbian' which are commonly used?

The term 'homosexual' is not nowadays sex specific. It was first used by Victorian scientists who regarded same-sex attraction and sexual behaviour as symptoms of mental disorders or moral deficiency. Homosexual men and women decided to use the term 'gay' in order to distance themselves from being labelled as somehow abnormal or ill. In fact, some people find the term 'homosexual' insulting and abusive and object to its use.

Generally, the terms 'gay' and 'lesbian' are seen as being less laden with negative implications than 'homosexual'. The term 'gay' is used to describe both homosexual men and lesbian women but has become particularly associated with homosexual men. Its derivation is unclear but may come from the nineteenth-century French slang for a homosexual man 'gaie'. Throughout the last century it has been used as a sort of code word between homosexual men.

However, in the late 1950s and 1960s it came into everyday use in association with the struggle for gay rights. In this context the word 'gay' came to represent, as it does now, a word with no negative connotations

but associated with a positive and proud sense of identity. Nowadays, the term 'lesbian' is used in relation to homosexual women and is derived from Lesbos, the name of the Greek island on which the lesbian poet Sappho lived in antiquity. In the past homosexual women have been called 'Sapphist' (again after Sappho). 'Straight' is used to describe heterosexual people and is an equivalent term to 'gay'.

Choosing which term to use and how to use it can be troubling. If a

> 'I don't mind so much what people call me as what they mean by it. I have been called a dizzy queen by some friends, and that's all right. But, mostly with people who are seriously prejudiced it's about how they say it – they say "gay" like it's a curse not something to be proud of.'
> Mark, 19

person is describing themselves they can be anxious about the reaction they might get. If a person is talking about someone else, or the issue in general, they can feel anxious about causing offence or saying the wrong thing.

Some men and women generally describe themselves as either 'gay' or 'straight'. Using these words gets away from the negative overtones of terminology like 'homosexual' or 'heterosexual' which for these people can feel too 'medical'. However, words like 'homosexual' and 'heterosexual' can have advantages in other contexts. Communication is a complex affair in which not only what words are used matters but also who is saying them, about whom and in what context.

For example, in school the term 'gay' is used a lot as an insult, and is not a word with positive overtones. A person called 'gay' by bullies in school might find it abusive because of the way it is said but the same person might happily call themselves 'gay' when they are with friends.

Defining homosexuality

How do you define homosexuality? Although the answer would appear to be simple, on closer examination it is more complex. People writing to magazine problem pages seem to define homosexuality using three criteria:

- having sexual feelings towards other people of the same sex;
- sexual behaviour with people of the same sex;
- and describing oneself as homosexual.

It can be helpful to think of these elements of a person's sexuality in a visual way. It is possible to conceive of sexual feelings, identity and behaviour as three circles which overlap to varying degrees depending on the individual.

Thinking first of sexual feelings and behaviour we can imagine a situation in which two different people might be represented by the diagrams below. In the first diagram the circles overlap about halfway. This person might be attracted to people of the same sex without acting on it – equally they might be having sex with people of the same sex but feeling like most of their sexual feelings are directed to people of the opposite sex. In the second diagram this person's sexual feelings and behaviour go together so that they feel attracted to people of the same sex and have sex with people of the same sex.

In the next situation, thinking of sexual feelings and identity, we can imagine how different people might be represented by these diagrams below. The first represents a person who is attracted to people of the same sex but does not always choose to call themselves gay. In the second diagram this person's sexual feelings and how they describe themselves are completely related.

Thinking of these diagrams it is clear that they could apply equally to defining homosexual or heterosexual behaviour. They also show that defining sexuality depends very much on the individual in question, their sexual feelings, behaviour and how they describe themselves. There is a wide spectrum of potential relationships between the three elements. In other words it can be

'I think that everyone is OK with the term "gay" nowadays. It says something about lifestyle and identity as well as sexual behaviour which homosexual doesn't seem to do. I describe myself as "straight" so I would use the word "gay" in the classroom. Anyway it's what the kids would say. But they do need to be clear about what all the terms mean otherwise telling off for being homophobic doesn't make any sense to them. They say, "it's just a word sir".'
Teacher

helpful to think of a spectrum of experience from exclusively homosexual to exclusively heterosexual with many people in between. Sometimes people who feel equally attracted to men and women and have sex with both, choose to place themselves in between and call themselves bisexual.

The main points to bear in mind when defining heterosexuality or homosexuality are:

- The three main factors are sexual attraction, sexual behaviour and identity. For most people the factors go together in a congruent way. So people tend to behave sexually in line with their sexual feelings, i.e. people tend to be sexually active with people they are attracted to.
- However, sexual identity and behaviour may be quite fluid over a period of time and they may not

always coincide with each other as people's feelings change. For example, a person may have at some point in their life a partner of the opposite sex and then later on someone of the same sex.

- Applying labels to people is not necessarily a good or accurate way of describing them. There may be phases in a person's life when their sexual feelings and behaviour are very clearly homosexual or heterosexual. However, at other times, labelling them as heterosexual or homosexual does not fit exactly with their sexual behaviour or feelings.

However, falling back on simple dichotomising definitions of homosexuality and heterosexuality can be appealing because it keeps the distinctions between them clear. Some common beliefs involve doing precisely this by showing homosexuality as a kind of reflection of heterosexuality. For example:

- Believing that some occupations and interests are more attractive and more suitable for heterosexual and others more attractive and suitable for homosexual people. For example, regarding sports as predominantly heterosexual and performing arts as homosexual.
- Assuming that when two lesbian women or two gay men are in a sexual relationship they will adopt roles which are traditionally masculine and feminine.

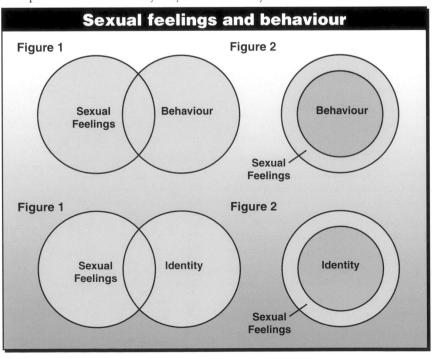

Sexual feelings and behaviour

Figure 1 — Sexual Feelings, Behaviour

Figure 2 — Behaviour, Sexual Feelings

Figure 1 — Sexual Feelings, Identity

Figure 2 — Identity, Sexual Feelings

- Believing that lesbian and gay people can be identified by the way they look and talk. Thinking, for example, that gay men look more effeminate than straight men and lesbian women look more masculine than straight women.

Any examination of homosexuality inevitably brings into the open implicit assumptions about what heterosexuality is. Stereotypes of heterosexuality and homosexuality and the rigid boundaries between them can be explored by asking questions like:
- Do a homosexual couple in love and a heterosexual couple in love experience the same feelings?
- If a person who calls themselves heterosexual has sex with someone of the same sex are they heterosexual, homosexual or bisexual?

- The above information is an extract from AVERT's web site which can be found at www.avert.org Alternatively see page 41 for their address details.

Homosexuality is . . .

Information from the Campaign for Homosexual Equality (CHE)

. . . wide-ranging

Sexuality involves feelings of attraction, having sex, loving people.

Sexuality with the same sex is described as homosexuality, in contrast to heterosexuality which is with the opposite sex.

These descriptions may seem useful in theory – but in real life it's not so simple:

– a married woman may be attracted to other women but have sex only with her husband;

– a happily married father may enjoy regular sex with another man.

To complicate matters, people who don't fit the popular image of their sex (e.g. boys who like cooking or girls who repair motor bikes) are sometimes labelled as homosexual.

In the end it's what people think of themselves that counts. Those of us who accept our homosexual feelings, or acknowledge that our homosexual feelings are stronger than our heterosexual ones, define ourselves as lesbians (gay women) or gay men.

As for lifestyles, gay people – just like heterosexual people – can be celibate, live in a partnership or sleep around. What else we do with our lives is just as varied!

. . . everywhere

You meet us every day: in your family, among your friends, at your place of work and in the street; but you don't see us!

We don't look any different so, unless we declare our sexuality, you won't know we're here.

If we don't tell you, it's because we're frightened that your reactions may be based on prejudice and ignorance.

If we 'come out', we can take part more fully in everyday life and have the same pride in our relationships as heterosexual people do.

If we don't 'come out' we have to live a double life, so we remain vulnerable to exposure and get no support if our relationships go through difficult patches. This leads to stress and unhappiness.

. . . surprising

Most people expect children to get married when they grow up. This assumes that everyone is heterosexual, an idea reinforced at school and by everything else around us, from soap adverts to soap operas. It

comes as a shock when this assumption is challenged.

Parents don't know how to react if their child is homosexual.

It's even more difficult for gay people: we learn to loathe homosexuality before we are aware that we are gay, so the discovery of our true feelings may make us feel isolated, lonely and despairing. Even when we have accepted our homosexuality, life can be difficult as everything from council houses to mail order catalogues assumes married couples are the only adults in the world!

Gay people need information, reassurance and support. Misinformation can cause great damage – for example, claims that homosexuality is a 'passing phase' can force people into marriage and cause unhappiness to others as well.

There's no way of telling if a child will grow up gay. It's no use looking for behaviour which doesn't fit the popular image of masculine or feminine – there's something of that in everyone!

. . . fighting prejudice

Many people fear an image of homosexuality which isn't based on reality. Some people assume that homosexuality is bad – without ever stopping to think why. These mistaken beliefs are often strengthened by sensational reports in newspapers or radio and television programmes.

As a result, people find themselves being treated differently just because they are (or they are suspected of being) gay:

- the law punishes gay people for behaviour which is acceptable in a heterosexual context;
- the State doesn't recognise gay relationships;
- their families may disown them;
- they get harassed at work and attacked in the street.

These inequalities give gay people the status of 'second-class citizens'.

... our experience

Pride:

Since the Campaign for Homosexual Equality began its work in 1969 we have seen real progress.

More liberal public attitudes now permit more varied lifestyles. This gives people freedom to behave in different ways.

As homosexuality is no longer taboo, it features more often in

magazines, newspapers, plays, films and on television. There has been a huge increase in the number of gay books, gay newspapers and gay magazines. Consequently, most large towns have meeting places for gay people and telephone information services.

Because we can now be more openly gay, we have a greater chance of fulfilment. We can now take pride in our love.

Injustice:

Things aren't perfect yet: gay people still have 'second-class' status.

We may be refused jobs or sacked simply because we're lesbian or gay.

We may lose custody of our children because gay people are considered unfit to be parents.

Unless we make special arrangements, we're not entitled to the same rights as heterosexual couples:

- we may not be allowed to visit our lovers in hospital;
- we may be thrown out of our homes when our lovers die.

• The Campaign for Homosexual Equality is working to bring lesbians and gay men the same rights in society as heterosexual people take for granted: will you help us? Please see page 41 for address details.

© *Campaign for Homosexual Equality (CHE)*

Section 28

Section 28 of the Local Government Act 1988 states that no local authority shall 'promote homosexuality' nor 'the acceptability of homosexuality as a pretended family relationship'. A move by the Labour government to repeal section 28 as part of the Local Government Bill was defeated in the House of Lords by 270-228 votes at the end of July 2000.

What is public opinion on section 28?

Results on the basis of gender:

Response	Total	Male	Female
The ban should remain	44%	55%	34%
The ban should end	54%	43%	64%
Don't know	2%	2%	2%

Results on the basis of children in household:

Response	Yes	No
The ban should remain	36%	48%
The ban should end	61%	50%
Don't know	3%	2%

Results on the basis of age:

Response	Total	15-24 years	25-44 years	46-64 years	65+ years
The ban should remain	44%	33%	32%	55%	60%
The ban should end	54%	66%	64%	44%	37%
Don't know	2%	1%	4%	1%	3%

What is happening in Scotland??

On 21 June 2000, the Scottish Parliament overwhelmingly passed the Ethical Standards in Public Life Bill, which included the repeal of section 28, by 99 votes to 17.

England and Wales are now the only countries in the world with a law like section 28.

In their consultation paper, the Scottish Executive stated that:

[. . .] this piece of legislation was, and remains, ill-conceived. Its existence has: served to legitimise intolerance and prejudice and, arguably, to raise the level of homophobia; acted as an unhelpful constraint on the ability of local authorities to develop best practice in sex education and bullying; and constrained the ability of local authorities to provide grants or funds to gay and lesbian groups in the community.

Source: Stonewall

Christianity and homosexuality

A short introduction from the Lesbian & Gay Christian Movement (LGCM)

What is homosexuality?

A crime in the UK? No longer as long as you are over 16, don't live on the Isle of Man (21) or Channel Isles (18), and do it in total privacy (but a recent court case makes this doubtful). These restrictions only apply to males as lesbians have never figured in the law of Britain.

A disease? – No, it's not, and you can't catch it either! Homosexuals do not need medical advice any more than heterosexuals do.

A homosexual is indeed a person who is attracted physically to another of the same sex. You may believe that sex has no other dimension than producing children. But if you move beyond this narrow vision of sex, you will know that it can give a richness and a depth to relationships which are founded on love. So a lesbian or gay man is not only a sexual being, but someone seeking to give love as well as receive it.

Our understanding of many things has changed and our understanding of sex is changing too.

The Lesbian & Gay Christian Movement needs and wants to be in the vanguard of these changes.

Some facts about homosexuality

Homosexuality is unusual but not unnatural. You could draw a parallel with being left-handed. A hundred years ago you would have been forced to be right-handed, but today it isn't a cause of active discrimination against you. And about one person in ten is predominantly homosexual in orientation. There are many more gay people in Britain than the whole population of Wales.

There is no real evidence to suggest that homosexuality is caused by emotional trauma, or a possessive mother, or an absent or unsympathetic father. Some psychiatrists claim that all their

homosexual patients are neurotic; but so are their heterosexual patients! Why else are they too on the couch?

High-minded moralists ask for strict laws to protect the young from homosexuals. But no greater proportion of homosexual men and women molest young children than do heterosexuals. The number is small. Some think that young people can be made into homosexuals, but no reputable psychiatrist would agree with this. What is more often needed is a friend or a counsellor to help a person clear away confusion about his or her sexual orientation. This can prevent the years of suffering and agony that people may otherwise have to endure before accepting the truth about themselves.

Can homosexuality be 'cured' or 'corrected'?

Young people who show 'homosexual tendencies' are often advised to get married and have a family; all will then be well, they are told. But these 'cure' marriages rarely, if ever,

work and they often end in tragedy, especially for the heterosexual partner and the children. A person needs to be sure that his or her homosexual behaviour is only very superficial before even thinking of marriage.

Rather, such young people need to be supported and respected in the process of trying to work through their doubts and insecurities about themselves. Without such acceptance and understanding, they may feel so threatened as to undergo extreme 'therapies', or to be 'exorcised' by misguided, albeit well-intentioned, Christians. This may temporarily change their behaviour, but dangerously blocks the facing of uncertainty which alone can lead to self-acceptance and the encouragement of responsible decisions about themselves. (These organisations are often called 'ex-gay', but frequently avoid this term in the face of critical publicity.)

Statement of conviction

It is the conviction of the members of the Lesbian & Gay Christian Movement that human sexuality in all its richness is a gift of God gladly to be accepted, enjoyed and honoured as a way of both expressing and growing in love, in accordance with the life and teaching of Jesus Christ. Therefore it is their conviction that it is entirely compatible with the Christian faith not only to love another person of the same sex but also to express that love fully in a personal sexual relationship.

• The above information is from the Lesbian & Gay Christian Movement's web site which can be found at www.lgcm.org.uk Alternatively see page 41 for address details.

Straights and gays take to same lifestyle

Are you gay, or does it just look as if you are? New research has revealed that gay and 'straight' lifestyles are becoming more alike.

The most detailed study of gay consumers reveals that heterosexuals are increasingly embracing gay culture, while homosexuals are emerging from gay ghettos to enjoy 'straight' lifestyles.

More than 10% of people who go to gay festivals such as Mardi Gras – Europe's largest gay festival, which takes place in London next month – are now heterosexual. And one in five drinkers, diners and clubbers who visit the so-called 'gay villages' in London, Manchester and Brighton are straight.

Only one-third of gays say they enjoy mixing with other gays in exclusively gay pubs and clubs. One in two prefers mixed venues. Three-quarters of gays reject holidays designed to cater for gays and choose mixed resorts and destinations.

Mintel, Britain's largest market research group, asked specialist market analysts ID Research to interview a representative sample of 1,000 people who attended the Mardi Gras festival last year. Researchers found that hit gay shows such as Channel Four's *Queer as Folk* and *Ellen* and the success of gay celebrities including Michael Barrymore, Graham Norton, and Anna Nolan in *Big Brother*, have broken down hostility towards homosexuals and popularised gay culture.

Jackie Robson, the report's author, said: 'There is a lot more tolerance towards gay lifestyles. It's normal to see gay characters on television or in the cinema and it is much easier to be openly gay in urban areas, especially London and Manchester, where the gay villages have developed. As these gay areas have grown and become fashionable they have become more popular with everyone – gay, straight or whatever.'

After years of proclaiming they were 'out and proud', the report says, gay people are embracing mainstream culture. 'Gays, especially the young, do not want to be seen as different any more. They want to be treated just like anyone else.'

More than 10% of people who go to gay festivals such as Mardi Gras – Europe's largest gay festival, which takes place in London – are now heterosexual

---

David Pinson, head of ID Research, says the findings confirm how attitudes to homosexuality have changed. 'Go back 10 or 20 years and being gay was difficult. You would segregate yourself not only so you could meet other gay people, but also to feel safe. But the world has changed. Gays have won important battles for equality and many now aspire to have their sexuality taken for granted.

'People like to be accepted as a member of the larger tribe. It is not hard. Gay people are fully aware of what a heterosexual lifestyle is because the whole social world continually creates and promotes it.'

In the pubs and bars of London's Soho last week, gay and straight drinkers backed the study's findings. Catherine, 38, who has been living with her girlfriend, Sara, for 10 years, said: 'I went away for a year in 1993 and when I came back, Soho was gay. Now it's full of straight people who cannot hold their drink and look messy. It's a nightmare when friends of mine go out on the pull.'

Tom, 28, drinking with his boyfriend Simon, said: 'Homophobia is still out there but at least gay pubs are more open. We've moved on from the clandestine gay bars of old, down side streets. Although there are still those who would rather keep the areas exclusively gay, I like the fact that straight people want to come to our bars. It promotes tolerance.'

Rachel, sitting with her boyfriend, Craig, goes to Old Compton Street to drink after work with her friends, most of whom are straight. 'In the big cities people don't care who you are or what you do. We are more accepting because if we weren't we wouldn't have any friends.

'The whole gay thing feels like the black thing was a few years ago. No one can remember what the fuss was all about. We are all too busy enjoying ourselves in whatever way feels right.'

By John Arlidge

• The above article appeared in the *Observer* on 27 May 2001.

Questions

Am I gay? Are you born gay? Can you stop being gay?

Am I gay?

Many people have feelings towards other people of the same sex, and wonder whether this means that they are gay. For many people these feelings can be very intense and alienating. Some people who are attracted to other people of the same sex are gay and go on to have sexual relationships with people of the same sex. But other people who have gay feelings find that these change over time and they become attracted to people of the opposite sex.

Other people are attracted to both men and women, and have relationships with both. Some people are not attracted to anyone and wonder if this is a sign of homosexuality. Often it is only time that will resolve these feelings. If you think you might be gay and feel you need to talk to someone most countries have telephone helplines and organisations that can provide information and support for you.

When do people know that they are gay?

There is no simple answer or standard answer to this question, as it varies from person to person. Generally it can be said that being gay is not something a person suddenly begins to consider, and it may not be something they can initially put a name to. Research published in 1996 showed how the young gay men interviewed had described a set of feelings which they gradually realised made them 'different' in some way, and a set of feelings they thought maybe every teenage boy has.

'I thought, well, this is just the phase bit. Sooner or later I'm going to start finding women attractive. I never did. As I became more attracted to men, and I still wasn't getting attracted to women, I thought, shit, you're gay. And it was really quite a shock when it hit me.'

Luke

Eventually all people who are gay realise that not only are they sexually attracted to members of the same sex, but that this attraction is not transitional. This realisation could come at any time during their lives.

Is homosexuality a phase young people go through?

For some people yes, and for others no. Some people do not have their first homosexual feelings or experience until they are well into adulthood. In a national survey in Britain carried out in the 1990s, nearly the same number of women reported their first homosexual experience had happened in their twenties as did in their thirties, forties or fifties. But, there is evidence that for some people homosexual experiences may well be part of a transitional or experimental phase in their youth. This is hardly surprising given that adolescence is a period of change in which many people find who they are and what they want for themselves in adult life. This kind of behaviour is perfectly normal.

Are you born gay? What causes people to be gay?

'One of the things I can remember thinking a lot about is . . . why am I like this? Is it someone's fault?'

Rob

There is no simple answer to the question, 'Are some people born lesbian or gay?' There are some theories which stress biological differences between heterosexual and homosexual adults, suggesting that people are born with their sexuality already determined.

In 1993 the American researcher Dean Hamer published research that seemed to prove that homosexual orientation could be genetically transmitted to men on the x chromosome, which they get from their mothers. However when this study was duplicated it did not produce the same results. A follow-up study which Hamer collaborated on also failed to reinforce his earlier results. Most recently research published in April 1999 by George Rice and George Ebers of the Universty of Western Ontario has cast doubt on Hamer's theory. Rice and Ebers' research also tested the same region of the x chromosome in a larger sample of gay men, but failed to find the same 'marker' that Hamer's research had produced. Claims that the part of the brain known as the hypothalamus is influential in determining sexual orientation, have yet to be substantiated. At the moment it is generally thought that biological explanations of sexuality are insufficient to explain the diversity of human sexuality.

'How can science tell you what I am? I mean I've had boyfriends, and was happy with them, had girlfriends and may have boyfriends again for all I know. If it's a gay gene what's going on? Is it just turning itself on and off in my head? It doesn't feel like biology it feels like love.'

Jo

Psycho-social explanations offer a variety of factors that could contribute to the development of a person's homosexuality. For example, a female-dominated upbringing in a gay man's past, with an absence of a male role model. Others stress adherence or deviance from conformity to gender roles, and individual psychological make-up. While none of these factors alone completely answers the question 'what causes homosexuality?', they rule out some things. For example, lesbian and gay young people are not 'failed' heterosexuals. Also, homosexual partners are generally of the same age proving wrong the assumptions that young people are 'turned gay' by older people.

What is clear is that people's behaviour is influenced by their family environment, their experiences and their sense of themselves. Beliefs about sex are initially shaped by family values. Later on these beliefs may be shaped by pleasant and unpleasant experiences of sex and also shape their choice of activities and partners. Throughout their life a person's sense of who and what they are has a strong impact on their sexual development and experience.

Can you stop being gay?

There is now growing general support for the belief that sexuality is pre-determined and may change over time, or remain fixed. However, many people are interested in whether sexuality can be altered solely by a person's desire to change. Organisations that help homosexuals attempt to change their sexuality can be generally divided between those that use psychological 'reparative' methods and those that use religious 'healing' methods.

Some people believe homosexuality is an illness and believe it can and should be cured. Many of these 'cures' revolve around psychological therapies (often called reparative therapy) which endeavour to re-orient a homosexual sexuality to heterosexual. Although there is little scientific data to evaluate, what is available seems to indicate that reparative therapy is ineffective. Last year the American Psychological

Association (APA), the world's largest association of psychologists, stated that:

'Homosexuality is not a mental disorder and the APA opposes all portrayals of lesbian, gay and bisexual people as mentally ill and in need of treatment due to their sexual orientation.'

Some strongly religious groups believe that homosexuality is sinful and is in direct breach of the Bible and other religious texts. As with reparative therapy there has been little to no scientific evaluation of the healing and prayer techniques used. What evidence is available suggests that the success of these techniques is restricted to three areas:

- Convincing bisexuals to limit their sexual activities to members of the opposite sex.
- Convincing homosexuals to become celibate.
- Convincing gay men and lesbians to attempt to maintain heterosexual relationships, whilst retaining their homosexual orientation.

Tellingly two founders of a ministry established to 'heal'

Some people believe homosexuality is an illness and believe it can and should be cured

---

homosexuals later described their programme as 'ineffective . . . not one person was healed'.

Recently the issue of changing homosexual orientation has been drawn into political debate in America. Although this is partly due to an issues shortage in American politics, the subject of 'curing' homosexuality has apparently captured the imagination of many Americans. Controversial full-page newspaper adverts by Christian political organisations have appeared three days in a row. The adverts, which firmly promote the theory that homosexuality can be changed through force of will alone, claim that 'thousands are leaving their homosexual identity for sexual celibacy, and even marriage'.

This appears to have been sparked from a speech by the Senate Majority leader in June 1998 that described homosexuals as people who are sick and can be cured – but only if they want to be. With the mid-term elections to Congress occurring in the autumn this could be a purely political move to make the president side with or against the American gay lobby.

• The above information is an extract from AVERT's web site which can be found at www.avert.org Alternatively see page 41 for their address details.

© AVERT

Coming out

Do you think you could be gay or bisexual? Do you know you are gay or bisexual? Information from Healthy Gay Scotland

Coming out is the term used for the act of telling another person that you are gay or bisexual. Coming out to yourself – accepting that you are gay or bisexual – is all part of the process.

For some people coming out can be straightforward, but for many it can be a confusing and stressful process. Gay and bisexual men often feel scared about coming out.

You may feel fine about coming out or you may be worried.

However you feel, we hope that you find this information useful. It is intended as a starting point and will hopefully lead you on to contacting others who can support you.

Advice from people who have gone through similar experiences can make the whole process of coming out much easier for you.

Coming out to yourself

Many of us have feelings for someone of the same sex. Some people may not understand this and get frightened, saying that it is bad or wrong. You may have been told that it is unnatural to be gay.

This is why it is sometimes difficult to come to terms with the fact that you may be gay yourself. It is important that you try to accept that there is nothing wrong with you. Your sexuality is a healthy part of you as a whole person.

Accepting that you are gay or bisexual can be a positive experience.

Coming out to others

Why come out to others?
Being gay or bisexual is nothing to be ashamed of. It is something which you can feel proud about and so it's natural that you will want to share that with others. It may be that you have a new boyfriend who you want to show off.

Remember that bottling up a secret can be very difficult. You may end up having to tell more and more lies to cover up your true feelings.

Healthy Gay Scotland

If you don't tell people who are close to you that you are gay, you may be cutting them off from a very important part of your life. It is difficult to keep a secret and can be very stressful.

Who are you going to come out to?
It's probably best to start with someone who you think will be more accepting. Are you prepared for a bad reaction? Are you prepared for a good reaction?

Should you come out in stages or all in one go?
This depends on you and how much support you have. Some people want to tell everyone at once and get it over with. Others come out over a number of years.

Who you tell is up to you. You may tell your best friend first or a member of your family. Remember to prepare yourself for both an adverse reaction and a good one. You are only being honest and telling someone the truth about yourself.

Should you come out to your parents?
Whether you have a close relationship with your parents or not, you may feel that this is an important part of your life that you want to share with them.

Some people find it easier to discuss the subject with one parent or another member of the family first before approaching the rest of the family.

How to do it

There is no right place or right time or right way to come out. It is best to try to avoid an argument about it, and of course it's best not to do it when you've had too much to drink. Try to plan ahead.

When coming out to someone, remember how long it has taken you to accept your sexuality. Others may need time to accept this also – so try to keep calm about it.

Here are some suggestions for responses to statements some people may make:

It's just a phase.
No. I've thought long and hard about this and it isn't.

It's not important.
It is to me. I've built up a lot of courage to tell you.

Was it something I did?
No. It's just the way I am.

God says it is wrong.
God made me the way I am.

Now it's said don't mention it again.
If I don't, I will have to lie about where I've been and who I see. I'm not willing to do that.

Why do you have to tell everyone about what you do in bed?
I'm not. I'm talking about my sexuality, which is different from sex. I'm telling you about me.

What's it like?
Here's what some people have said about their experience.

'*My mum cried and said she would never have grandchildren and she would never accept it. Now she's been to gay bars with me, met my friends and she's as proud of me as I am of her.*'
Jason, 18

'*My parents' biggest regret was that I hadn't told them sooner. They were hurt that I was afraid to share my life with them.*'
Liam, 20

'*I remember thinking that the family get-together at Christmas would be the best place to bring up the issue. So plucking up all my courage I said, "Mother, would you please pass the salt to a homosexual". She passed it to my father. A terrible scene ensued.*'
Paul, 16

'*My friend said it wasn't news, everyone had guessed already, and didn't I know that.*'
Mike, 18

'*It took me years to come to terms with my own sexuality but somehow I expected my parents to shout for a day, cry for a week and then get over it. It takes time and patience.*'
David, 19

'*I became closer than I thought I could to my friends.*'
Danny, 16

'*I came out of the closet in the worst way I think was possible. I was having a storming argument with my mother because she wanted me to buy a suit for a job interview and I wanted to wear something different. I told her that she didn't understand me and that I was different. She asked what I meant and I shouted "I'm gay". She stood quietly for a second and then said, 'I think I should call your father'. Of course there was the usual stuff about it being a phase and that I would get over it, was it something they had done, was I just saying it to spite them. They're great now, but it took a while for them to get used to the idea and to get to know me for who I am. I now have a really good relationship with them – at least it's honest.*'
John, 20

• The above information is an extract from the Healthy Gay Scotland web site which can be found at www.hgscotland.org.uk See page 41 for further address details.
© Healthy Gay Scotland

Sex education

Information from Stonewall

The Education Reform Act 1988 requires that the national curriculum promote the spiritual and moral development of pupils to prepare them for adult life. The revised National Curriculum was published last year.

The new statutory sex and relationship guidance published in July 2000 has a section dealing with the needs of young lesbians and gay men – the first time ever that gay sexuality has been recognised.

How does the new National Curriculum treat sexuality?
The revised National Curriculum was published last year. The Education Reform Act 1988 requires that the national curriculum will: 'promote the spiritual and moral development of pupils and [to] prepare them for the opportunities and responsibilities of adult life'.

These curriculum requirements

are interpreted and further guidance is provided in subsequent sections about Key Stages 3 and 4 (age 11-16 years).

The Education Act 1996 requires the Schools Inspectorate to inspect and evaluate schools' provision for spiritual and moral development.

Personal, social and health education is an aspect of the requirement on the national curriculum to provide spiritual, moral and cultural education. The new guidelines for Key Stage 3, published in 1999, suggest pupils should be taught *inter alia*:

• In a context of the importance of relationships, about human reproduction, contraception, sexually transmitted infections, HIV and high-risk behaviours including early sexual activity;
• To recognise and manage risk and make safer choices about healthy lifestyles;
• To recognise when pressure from others threatens their personal safety and well-being and to develop effective ways of resisting pressures, including knowing when and where to get help;
• About the effects of all types of stereotyping, prejudice, bullying, racism and discrimination and how to challenge them assertively;
• How to empathise with people different from themselves;
• About the role and importance of marriage in family relationships;

- About the role and feeling of parents and carers and the value of family life.

This sort of approach is also reflected in the Government's new Healthy Schools Standard Initiative.

At Key Stage 4 (14-16-year-olds) the new guidelines suggest *inter alia* that pupils should be taught:

- About the diversity of different ethnic groups and the power of prejudice;
- To work co-operatively with a range of people who are different from themselves;
- About the nature and importance of marriage for family life and bringing up children;
- About the role and responsibility of a parent and the qualities of good parenting and its value to family life.

The Secretary of State for Employment and Education has made it clear that the Government places considerable emphasis on the importance of marriage in family relationships and parenting.

Who decides what can and cannot be taught in sex education?

The Education Reform Act 1988 placed the responsibility for sex education in the hands of governors. However, the responsibility for other areas of the curriculum rests with the Head Teacher. The Act sets out the overall requirements of the curriculum. S1 requires schools to offer a curriculum which:

a. promotes the spiritual, moral, cultural, mental and physical development of pupils at school and of society; and

b. prepares such pupils for the opportunities, responsibilities and experiences of adult life.

Section 28 is largely irrelevant to questions concerning the teaching of homosexuality in schools. As explained above sex education is in the hands of the governors and overall responsibility for the curriculum resides with the Head Teacher. Section 28 only applies to local authorities and local education authorities. The responsibility of local education authorities is now only to publish and keep under review their policy on secular provision and

consider the range and balance of the curriculum.

How does homosexuality fit into sex education?

The answer to this question is quite easy – homosexuality fits into education the same way as heterosexuality does.

The Department of Education Circular 5/94 states:

'the purpose of sex education should be to provide knowledge about loving relationships, the nature of sexuality, and the processes of human reproduction'.

The Sex Education Forum divides the term sexuality into three parts: sexual orientation, sexual behaviour and sexual identity.

According to the Sex Education Forum:

sexual orientation refers to a person's primary sexual attraction, be it to the same, opposite or both sexes;

sexual behaviour refers to what a person does sexually; and

sexual identity refers to how people see themselves and present themselves to others.

Obviously, sex education is failing in its attempts 'to provide

---

In general, issues of sexuality should always be addressed accurately, honestly and non-judgementally

---

knowledge about loving relationships' and the 'nature of sexuality' if it is exclusively heterosexual.

How can issues of sexuality be addressed at school?

In general, issues of sexuality should always be addressed accurately, honestly and non-judgementally, keeping in mind that all students have the moral and legal right to expect that the school will attend to their needs.

Key to addressing issues of sexuality at school is ensuring that teachers are adequately educated on the issues themselves. Teachers should become aware of the prevalence of homophobia and its implications and should be taught to avoid stereotyping, once again in the spirit of attending the needs of all students.

The Sex Education Forum (1995, p. 3) offers these suggestions on addressing issues of sexuality:

- Challenge the behaviour or statement rather than the opinion, belief or whole person. Acknowledge and accept diverse cultural and ethnic beliefs;
- Avoid polarising the situation by countering homophobic remarks with an opposing view. A more productive approach would give pupils an opportunity to examine the 'offending' viewpoint. For example, 'I can understand why you have that view considering media coverage of this issue but let's talk about how someone might feel if you called them that.'

- Challenge myths and offer a different perspective;
- Use helping or counselling skills such as open questions to draw out discussion;
- Learn to recognise people's ability to deny or their refusal to accept others' beliefs, activities and orientations;
- Always try and bring the situation to a conclusion. Do not bring up these issues towards the end of a lesson. Allow pupils time to consider the situation or statement, explore the effect of possible outcomes and plan the best way forward;
- Ensure that everyone who wants to speak can do so. If necessary remind pupils of the ground rules: 'We said that we would listen to each other.' Encourage everyone to speak by asking pupils to work in pairs or small groups;

What does Stonewall think about sex education?

We believe that sex education, like all other teaching, has to be inclusive. The new statutory Sex and Relationship Guidance clearly emphasises stable relationships – some of our fiercest opponents in the Lords have complained that they only mention marriage three times. There is now no excuse for schools to duck the issue or fail to take steps to provide information and guidance on homosexuality.

- Intervene when you hear personal attacks;
- Use classroom activities which encourage empathy, for instance ask pupils to think and imagine what it would feel like to have certain experiences;

- If you know or suspect that someone is being harassed or bullied, talk with the young person at the end of the lesson;
- Be prepared for pupils to approach you at the end of the lesson. Be supportive, have details of outside agencies that could help.

Other suggestions include:
- Inviting guest speakers (especially former students)
- Lead open discussions concerning the oppression of lesbians and gay men
- Teach literature and/or plays with a lesbian or gay theme

• The above information is an extract from information on Stonewall's web site. For further information, see their web site at www.stonewall.org.uk Alternatively, see page 41 for Stonewall's address details.

© Stonewall

Calling for honesty in education

Information from the Campaign for Homosexual Equality (CHE)

Homosexuality is a fact of life

Throughout history there have been women who loved women and men who loved other men. People don't need sex education to tell them how to fall in love: it's a natural feeling that develops inside them. Gay men and women become aware of these feelings in the same way that heterosexual women and men do – but, gay or straight, the experience is different for everyone.

Some children have recognised their homosexuality before entering secondary school, others become increasingly aware of it during their teens when sexual feelings begin to be expressed more often and discussed more openly.

Homosexual pupils have the same need for a relationship as their heterosexual friends do – but the chances are they won't find one so easily; heterosexuality is forced on everyone and homosexuality is ignored (or, worse, forbidden).

In spite of this, many lesbians and gay men meet people with whom to share their lives. They find love, happiness and fulfilment in a number of ways. Now that homosexual relationships are increasingly accepted, more people are able to live the kind of life that suits them best.

Society is all the better for this: modern life creates enough stress without adding the extra burden of trying to hide the essential part of our personality, so the freedom to be oneself avoids the kinds of breakdown that result in extra demands on the social services.

Sadly, there is still a noisy minority which tries to stir up ill-feeling against homosexual relationships. Their 'arguments' are based on their own emotions, not the real facts: most of them are religious fundamentalists who claim that homosexuality is 'against God's laws'. In fact, they regularly ignore many of the other 'laws' found in sacred writings, so their position is rather hypocritical. What's more, even within the various Christian denominations in this country there is no agreed opinion on homosexuality. The fundamentalists are a minority within minorities.

For those who see homosexuality as a medical 'problem' rather than a religious issue, the arrivals of AIDS has provided an emotional prop to a crumbling argument. But we all know – or should do if the Government publicity campaign has had any effect – that AIDS is not restricted to homosexual people. Indeed, lesbians are least likely of anyone to be infected with the HIV virus.

Objections to homosexual relationships rely on emotion, not reason: the facts actually argue in favour of allowing people to express their own homosexuality. Everyone has a right to be accepted on their own terms by other people. People who might express 'disgust' about homosexuality are making a statement about their own ignorance and emotions, not about the reality of homosexual relationships – many of them would be surprised to know what their neighbours do, but they wouldn't condemn them. Variation is accepted – as long as it's heterosexual!

Why should homosexuality be treated any differently? It's only another aspect of this variation. Nobody has any right to limit another person's liberties, unless these can be shown (not just imagined) to harm others.

Negative images

It could be argued that there is no need for education about personal relationships: our own emotions and the examples set by other people should guide us through life. But emotions can't always be trusted and the examples we see around us may not be appropriate.

Homosexual people are at a particular disadvantage when they look around for suitable examples to follow: although they will see all kinds of heterosexual relationships, either among the people they know or in films, plays and on television, they won't find much about homosexual relationships.

What kind of picture would you have developed about heterosexual relationships if you hadn't grown up in a heterosexual society but had to rely on stories in newspapers?

That's what gay people have to contend with: their first information about homosexuality comes from heterosexual people and is usually distorted by ignorance and prejudice. Newspaper stories concentrate on the seamy side of life, so people who rely on them get a distorted view of the world. The good sides of homosexual relationships never hit the headlines. Popular images of homosexuality are therefore negative ones.

Most children have picked up these negative images of homosexuality by the time they leave primary school: they've learnt to tell jokes about 'queers', shout 'lezzie' or 'pouff' at people they don't like, and they've heard stories about what gay people are thought to do for sex. But they don't actually know anything – all the information they receive is gossip. They've picked up the negative images of homosexuality before they even know what sexuality is.

For people growing up gay, the constant exposure to negative images is a great disadvantage: it undermines their self-confidence and creates conflict between what they know about homosexuality through their own experience and what they learn from other sources. Until they can meet other lesbian/gay people they are unable to discover the positive side of the picture that will help them to develop their own personality fully.

One of the aims of Health Education, stated several times in *Health Education from 5 to 16*, is to foster the self-esteem of pupils. How can this be done if health educators remain silent about homosexuality and fail to counteract the false information that pupils pick up in the playground?

Positive images

A society which claims to be unbiased must make sure its members see every side of the situation. Most information about homosexuality is so biased by the heterosexual perspective that it fails to give people any idea of the everyday life of lesbians and gay men.

This heterosexual bias is sometimes called heterosexism and, like any one-sided argument, prevents people from discovering the real truth. Unless health education courses make a positive effort to provide a counterbalance to heterosexual bias, they will do nothing to help lesbian and gay pupils develop the self-confidence they need for mature relationships. Furthermore, the courses will fail to meet the final objective of health education set out in *Health Education from 5 to 16*:

'With regard to skills pupils should know how to distinguish between fact, promotion and polemic, and how to weigh and interpret information and evidence about health from a variety of sources; that is, they should be able to analyse data in table form and in simple graphs; comment critically on health-

related material (such as advertisements); be able to locate information which relates to health and safety and to personal lifestyles and have acquired the knowledge base and developed the confidence in themselves to begin to make choices about health based on evidence.'

But it isn't just the homosexual pupils who will benefit from positive images of homosexuality in a sex education course. The Government publication also says that health education 'should cultivate a respect for others, an understanding of different lifestyles...', so it is clear that heterosexual pupils should be given sufficient insight into homosexual relationships to respect them. Too many heterosexual people are ignorant about homosexuality, which is why it causes them problems at times – as, for instance, when parents discover one of their children is lesbian/gay.

Much of the hostility towards gay men and women results from fear. Fear grows from ignorance and can lead to violence. Attacks on lesbians and gay men are intolerable in a civilised society – indeed, *Health Education from 5 to 16* makes it clear that schools should 'cultivate an abhorrence of both physical and mental cruelty'. But violence is a primitive response to the unknown, so the only way to fulfil this objective is to ensure that ignorance is wiped out.

A few people have campaigned in public to criticise schools and Local Education Authorities which intend to adopt positive images of homosexuality in their sex education courses. These critics are not only blind to the heterosexual bias in society, but some of them actually misrepresent these policies as an attack on heterosexuality instead of an attempt to overcome heterosexism. A few even claim that the policies are designed to 'promote homosexuality' – but is sexuality such a flimsy part of out nature? Even when homosexuality was never mentioned, there were plenty of homosexual women and men in society. They couldn't have been affected by positive images – they knew what they were without them!

Which brings us back to the purpose of sex education. It is not a set of instructions which everyone is expected to follow. Sex education is an exploration of possibilities which should train pupils in the skill of decision-making and, at the same time, actually help them to decide their own future.

Discrimination against any minority is both socially divisive and unfair

---

If this is to be done properly and responsibly, there must be no hiding of facts or giving partial information. Each school has a duty to eliminate bias, whatever the personal views of its teachers or the principles upon which it was founded. The Government booklet makes this quite clear:

'It is recognised that individual teachers have views of their own about these matters and that often pupils will want to know, and seek to find out, where the teachers stand. Given that pupils are apt to place great weight upon what their teachers say in these matters, teachers have to set out their own views with the utmost care while pointing out that other people, including the pupils' own parents, might sincerely and properly hold quite different views.'

Conclusion

A great deal of unnecessary fuss is made about homosexuality. In *Health Education from 5 to 16* it is classed as a 'sensitive issue' and described as 'difficult territory for teachers to traverse'. This betrays the heterosexual bias of the booklet's authors and reinforces the mystery surrounding the subject.

The time has come to break down the barriers of ignorance and treat homosexuality with the matter-of-fact approach it deserves. Any attempts to block such openness must be resisted fiercely: an overwhelming majority of people in this country accept homosexual relationships as a fact of life yet a tiny minority opposed to this view is trying to impose its beliefs on us all. Their arguments are deceitful and smack of the 'Big Brother' mentality.

It's not enough to ignore homosexuality: prejudice still makes life difficult for lesbians and gay men. The only way to combat this is to make sure everyone knows the full facts about homosexuality – the good side, not just the bad. In other words, to adopt a 'positive images' policy wherever possible.

Discrimination against any minority is both socially divisive and unfair. Any move to prevent people showing support for homosexuals in our society is discriminatory and should therefore be opposed. Once one minority has been singled out in this way, which will be the next?

• The above information is an extract from *Homosexuality – Calling for Honesty in Education*, produced by the Campaign for Homosexual Equality. See page 41 for their address details.

© Campaign for Homosexual Equality.

Homosexuality

Information from the Scottish Catholic Media Office

A distinction must be made between tendency and act. Having a tendency or predisposition to behave in a certain way does not justify giving expression to it. For example, anger: I am not entitled to vent my anger as and when I please simply because I have that tendency. The same principle applies to heterosexual sex.

- Homosexual sex can never be procreative. Sex which divorces the loving, affirmative aspect from the procreative aspect converts such intercourse into an end in itself. In this respect, the Church does not apply different standards to single people of either sexual orientation: the natural context for sex is within marriage, always open to new life.

- One can love another person of the same sex very deeply without having sex; in fact, there are many ways of expressing one's love that do not involve sex at all. Celibacy, for instance, calls both homosexuals and heterosexuals to a life of chastity. Not having sex does not lead to an inferior quality of life.

- One of the characteristics of the emergence of 'gay culture' has been the encouragement of the high level of promiscuity which, for various reasons, is a feature of male homosexuality the world over. Long-term, stable and single partner homosexual partnerships, although they do exist, are comparatively rare: 74% of male homosexuals reported having more than 100 partners during their lifetime, 65% reported having sex only once with more than half their partners, 28% reported having more than 1000 partners, 10% of homosexuals and 28% of lesbians claim to be quasi married (cf. Bell & Weinberg, *Homosexualities: A Study of Diversity among Men and Women*, New York: Simon & Schuster, 1978: 308,346).

- In Denmark a form of homosexual marriage has been legalised since 1989. By 1995, fewer than 5% of Danish homosexuals had married and 28% of these 'marriages' had already ended in 'divorce' or death. (Wockner, *Advocate*, 726 4 Feb. 1997: 26)

- Human beings are not defined by their sexual orientation. Homosexual people, as human beings, have the same rights as others – including that of not being treated in a manner which offends their personal dignity.

- The Church is compassionate to people with this tendency and recognises the considerable numbers who struggle to come to terms with it. She seeks to bring the person to a greater fulfillment and healing, and a more profound understanding of the self. 'Homosexual activity prevents one's own fulfilment and happiness by acting contrary to the creative wisdom of God. The Church, in rejecting erroneous opinions regarding homosexuality, does not limit but rather defends personal freedom and dignity realistically and authentically understood' (Congregation for the Doctrine of the Faith, *Letter to the Bishops of the Catholic Church on the Pastoral Care of Homosexual Persons*, 1986).

Notes
Catechism of the Catholic Church 2357
'Pastoral Care of Homosexuals', by Fr Jean Louis Brugues OP, *Observatore Romano*, March 1997, (available on Alapadre Catholic Web Site www.alapadre.net)
Publications of Family and Youth Concern 01865 351966

Prejudice and discrimination

Poll shows prejudice rife as Stonewall launches new project to combat discrimination

A new MORI poll on attitudes to minority groups released today shows England still has a long way to go to become an inclusive, tolerant society, warned Stonewall, the national organisation working for social equality and legal justice for lesbians, gay men and bisexuals.

The poll found that almost two-thirds of people in England (64%) can name at least one minority group towards whom they feel less positive – representing 25 million adults across the country. The most frequently cited groups are travellers/gypsies (35%), refugees and asylum seekers (34%), people from a different ethnic group (18%) and gay or lesbian people (17%).

Prejudice against one group often goes hand in hand with prejudice against others. People who are prejudiced against any ethnic minority are twice as likely to be prejudiced against gay or lesbian people (33% compared to 17%). They are four times as likely to be prejudiced against disabled people (8% compared to 2%).

Knowing someone who is gay or lesbian, or someone from a different ethnic group, reduces by half the likelihood of prejudice against those groups.

And there is evidence of widespread acceptance of gay and lesbian people: overall, 63% said they would feel comfortable with a gay or lesbian GP, and 62% with a gay or lesbian teacher. 73% of people with children in their household would be comfortable with a gay or lesbian teacher.

The survey was commissioned by Citizenship 21, a new Stonewall initiative launched today, aimed at combating discrimination.

The project was born as a direct result of the nail bombings which targeted different minority communities in London in 1999, killing three people. Backed by a £900,000 grant from the Community Fund (announced last year), Citizenship

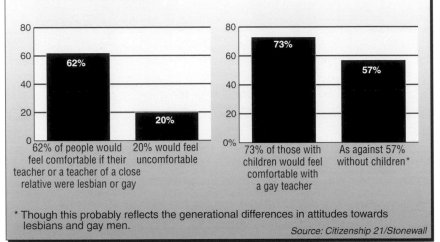

Attitudes to lesbians and gay men

Commissioned by Stonewall's Citizenship 21 Project, new data from a MORI poll reveal the profile of prejudice in this country. The survey confirms positive signs regarding attitudes to lesbians and gay men. An analysis of the responses on attitudes to lesbians and gay men as teachers, an area which was the subject of great controversy during the debate on Section 28.

62% of people would feel comfortable if their teacher or a teacher of a close relative were lesbian or gay | 20% would feel uncomfortable

73% of those with children would feel comfortable with a gay teacher | As against 57% without children*

* Though this probably reflects the generational differences in attitudes towards lesbians and gay men.

Source: Citizenship 21/Stonewall

21 will provide grants to community groups, and information, training and research to help build links between communities and tackle prejudice.

Knowing someone who is gay or lesbian, or someone from a different ethnic group, reduces by half the likelihood of prejudice against those groups

---

Angela Mason, executive director of Stonewall, said: 'This survey gives us new insights into the profile of prejudice in this country. There clearly are a number of factors which predispose people to dislike and fear others who are different. There is "joined-up prejudice" and we need new "joined up" responses. Racism and homophobia, for instance, very often go together.'

'Citizenship 21 is about providing that joined-up response. It is a practical way of challenging prejudice by offering resources for those who want to work together for equality.'

Lady Diana Brittan, chair of the Community Fund, said:

'The Community Fund's award to Stonewall for the Citizenship 21 Project came out of the tragic nail bombings in London in 1999. This highlighted the need for a common approach towards overcoming all forms of prejudice. I hope that our grant will build bridges between vulnerable communities and this project will bring about a more tolerant society.'

• The MORI results are based on responses from 1,183 adults aged 15+, interviewed by MORI face to face, in home, using self-completion questionnaires. Interviews were conducted at 167 sampling points across England, between 24 and 30 May 2001. Data are weighted to the known national population profile.

© MORI (Market & Opinion Research International Limited)

Prejudice against gay men

Attitudes to gay men and homophobia. Information from AVERT

What is homophobia?

Sometimes people who object to gay people are called homophobic. Homophobia is a fear of and/or hostility towards gay people or homosexuality. Homophobia is often expressed visibly, audibly and sometimes violently. Research carried out in 1996 by gay rights group Stonewall showed that gay people had experienced more extreme homophobia as young people than as adults. The research found that as young people 90% of the respondents had been called names and nearly 50% had been violently attacked. In areas of England homophobic bullying in schools has now reached the point where young people being bullied have special homework clubs.

Attitudes to gay men

Although people often grow up exposed to more or less the same beliefs about sexuality, they can hold quite different attitudes in their adult lives. While some people believe homosexuality is a valid lifestyle, others violently object. Some people believe that homosexuality is unnatural, others see it as a sin and have said that for gay men 'AIDS is a plague sent from God'.

At the beginning of the AIDS epidemic, gay men were frequently singled out for abuse as they were deemed to be responsible for the cause and spread of the virus. Sensational reporting in the press became progressively anti-gay and did little to help the situation. One prominent gay activist was attacked outside a London subway by a gang of knife-wielding youths who suggested that he should be killed before he could spread 'the gay plague' to others.

In contrast the current UK Labour Government has a gay front-bench minister, as well as several gay back-benchers. Part of this government's mandate is to address the age of consent for gay men during the current Parliament, as well as review the ban on gay men and lesbians serving in the army.

What causes people to be prejudiced against gay men and lesbians?

There are probably no simple causes of homophobia. While there is probably no single thing which causes a person to be homophobic, research has shown that prejudice towards gay people and homosexuality can be influenced by the person:

- Reporting no homosexual experiences or feelings.
- Being negative about types of sexual behaviour and relationships which are neither procreative nor take place within marriage.
- Having a lower educational and social status, for example the lower a person's level of educational attainment and social class the more negative their attitudes are towards homosexuality.
- Having and adhering to strong religious beliefs which disapprove of sex and/or homosexuality.
- Having little/no social contact with lesbian and gay people.

'When you're scared, especially of something you actually know nothing about, hatred is a natural reaction.'
Robert, 25

Prejudice among young people

Amongst young people, boys and girls who do not act in line with their gender stereotype – for example boys being sporty, strong decision-makers and girls being more emotional, expressive nurturers – may be subjected to severe bullying. This may include accusations of being of the opposite sex, or of being gay. Boys who show their feelings or who are too intimate with other boys are often called 'girls' or 'poofs'. Girls who are deemed to be too boyish or who hold feminist views run the risk of being called 'dykes' or 'lesbians'.

Boys may be more prejudiced than girls towards gay people. This is because the boundaries on boys' gender roles are much more rigid than they are for girls. As a result boys have a limited number of ways acceptable to their peer group to express their emotions. This often means that any expression between boys may be seen by their peers as latent homosexual interest. Between girls, in contrast, close friendships which involve embracing, touching and sharing thoughts and feelings are more legitimate and are less likely to be seen by their peers as an indication of homosexuality.

Gay and other less flattering words are often used by young people as standard insults. This derogatory use of words associated with homosexuality is one way in which young people learn it is highly undesirable to be gay. This can have a number of effects.

- It silences young people who are experiencing gay feelings.
- In order to protect themselves young gay men often pretend to be heterosexual and sometimes join in homophobic taunts themselves.

'I was waiting and expecting to hear something about homosexuality, safe sex and different things in sex education. Maybe some information that could help me. But I got nothing.'
Tim

- The atmosphere at school reinforces the isolation of young people who are being bullied or abused because they are perceived to be gay – there is no one to talk to and people are very hesitant to defend them.
- Gay young people are kept separate from each other

because of the implications of being seen together by their peers.

Many gay and lesbian adults say that they began to identify themselves as 'different' in their secondary school

years. In this period, the absence of support, understanding or information was sometimes a source of distress in itself and often magnified their anxieties.

• The above information is an extract from AVERT's web site which can be found at www.avert.org

Background to homophobia

What are the thinking, feeling and behaviour of a homophobic person in a social environment

Q. What does this word 'homophobia' mean?

A. Homophobia is the irrational hatred and fear of people who are attracted to the same sex that is nurtured by institutionalised biases in a society or culture.

In brief, homophobia is a nurtured (learnt) condition influenced by these six key aspects of our society:

1. Religion – Religious conviction may be used as a pretext for violent homophobic attacks.
2. Education – There has been a failure to address homophobia and a lack of available information on Personal, Health and Social Education.
3. Politics – There has been slow progress politically to address the law reforms on equality, given the climate of homophobia.
4. Family pressures – Parents who hold homophobic views tend to promote an exclusively heterosexual lifestyle.
5. Acquaintances – Young gays tend to see 98% of their fellows as homophobic.
6. Individuals – Outside pressures lead to self-doubt and an inability to accept one's own sexual identity because of feelings of guilt and isolation.

Religion stumbles with nurture instead of nature

Throughout history religions have been the main promoters of anti-gay misinformation and propaganda to the masses. Questionable interpreta-

GAYTEENS.ORG

tion of doctrine and even inaccurate translation have indirectly led to suffering and harm to those who are perceived to transgress. In this context religious institutions have failed in their educative role. Particularly pernicious have been the religious and psychiatric schools of thought which have taught that homosexuality is acquired rather than inborn, and have attempted to alter individuals' sexuality through clinical, psychological or religious means. There is now documentary evidence to show that this view is dangerously mistaken. Homophobia is, however, an acquired condition heavily influenced by upbringing and environment.

Homophobic people often assert that homosexuals have the choice of not being homosexual; that is, we don't have to act out our sexual identity

Education – politics interfering with education

The schoolteacher has as important a role as the parent in safeguarding the mental and physical welfare of their young charges. The desire to educate young people in the actualities of social and family structures and normal sexual development, which should have the effect of reassurance on adolescents exploring their own sexual orientation, is frustrated by the insistence of society on the perpetuation of a mythological world view which either denies the possibility of homosexual love or sees it simply as dangerous, sinful and unviable. Some teachers are unfortunately unable to prevent their personal feelings and prejudices from influencing their approach to these subjects, and the mistreatment of youngsters seen as sexually different by not only their peers but also their teachers can lead to misery, isolation, and even suicide within the very institutions charged to protect them. Legal restrictions such as Section 28 in the UK also prevent teachers from supplying a balanced range of information, particularly in the field of sexual health, and may lead to a climate of fear, which deters school children from seeking pastoral help when they most need it.

Politics – the perceived threat to accepted values

Anyone who does not adopt a society's usual value system runs the risk of being seen as undermining the society, because the person does not share the interests and goals of the majority.

The debates over Section 28 and the minimum gay age of consent represent the latest attempt by governments to address inequality even within the climate of homophobia. Politicians have made progress and a contribution to the homophobia debate.

The Labour government has attacked homophobia in a series of high profile initiatives and achieved success and new respectability for gay human rights issues. Members of the government themselves can now be honest about their sexuality without fear of reprisal, and can set the pattern for the society they represent.

Further reforms are planned: the recognition of gay marriages, the institution of further employment rights, and the imposition by the judiciary of harsher sentences on those convicted of crimes against ethnic and sexual minorities, where there is evidence that a particular crime was motivated by hatred.

The family

Our parents are influenced by their society/culture, their own parents, education, religion and government laws; these influence and reinforce the bias from generation to generation.

Many parents, because of their natural desire for the continuation of their bloodline, find it difficult to come to terms with their gay child and prefer to avoid discussion, leaving their children to suffer alone in silence. Parents continue to brainwash their children into believing that they must conform to the accepted heterosexual pattern.

Acquaintances and friends

Individuals will hide their sexuality from those around them for fear of losing friendships by arousing reactions of fear and, paradoxically, envy, since they may be seen to be evading the responsibilities and expense of parenthood through their chosen lifestyle.

Individuals' own fears

It is not surprising that many gay

people resort to suicide to escape depression and failure and to cope with isolation and fear. A particularly poignant case was that of Darran Steele: in March 1998 this 15-year-old school boy hanged himself in Burton, Staffordshire, UK. According to research some leaders of the homophile movement believe that the most vociferous enemies of homosexuals are combating homosexual urges in themselves. Their confusion and anger can lead to violent and even homicidal outbursts, as in the cases of the Admiral Duncan Gay Bar bombing and the December 1997 shooting at Heath High School in West Paducah, Kentucky, which left three students dead and five wounded.

Many parents, because of their natural desire for the continuation of their bloodline, find it difficult to come to terms with their gay child

---

Solutions to homophobia

Religions need to be more tolerant and accepting and to reform those of their teachings that promote homophobia. Homosexuality must be given equality with heterosexuality or religion will decline in its relevance to society.

The educational establishment needs to dispel present fears through the promotion of sexual equality and

of understanding and acceptance within its own institutions, using tools such as the Internet. Voluntary institutions such as gay youth groups should work in conjunction with schools.

Government needs to continue to reform laws and introduce new laws to protect individuals from inequality.

Parents need to be re-educated in the true nature of homosexuality and the dangers their homophobic beliefs may create for their children.

Classmates and peers can be educated to be more sensitive to the problems of sexual identity experienced by their fellows.

Society and its minorities

The perceived wisdom of our society, with its roots in Christian culture, leaves little room for aberration from the norm, and tends to reinforce homophobic thought and behaviour. Young children are taught to conform, and this is a particularly potent pressure at puberty, when the importance of preparation for marriage and procreation is instilled, and adolescents aware of their 'deviant' sexuality become increasingly isolated, particularly when subjected to verbal and physical bullying by their peers. Because of the negative attitude toward homosexuality which has permeated our culture, the process of coming to terms with one's same-sex attraction has often involved the development of two social identities: the carefully constructed and self-consciously maintained 'closeted' one of heterosexuality for the general public, and the emerging and fragile gay identity among one's peers.

Homophobia is an attitude held by many non-homosexuals and also it can be also held by the majority of homosexuals in countries where there is discrimination against homosexuals. Heterosexism creates the climate for homophobia with its assumption that the world is and must be heterosexual and its display of power and privilege is the norm. Homophobic people often assert that homosexuals have the choice of not being homosexual; that is, we don't have to act out our sexual identity, but should be content with the trappings of heterosexual social interconnections and heterosexual privilege.

Conclusion

Here we have a summary of the cycle of homophobia that is alive and active among us in society. It is a learnt disorder and highly dangerous in our society, in that it divides families, creates discord and makes misery for millions.

• Gayteens Resources offers global support and information for young people, families and those unsure of their sexuality. The site is dedicated to Darran Steele (15) and Robbie Kirkland (14) and the thousands who have attempted or committed suicide because of society's failure to address homophobia.

• The above information is an extract from information on the Gay Teens web site which can be found at www.gayteens.org

Fury over gay study

Professor condemned as he suggests some homosexuals can go straight

Some gay people can turn heterosexual if they are highly motivated to do so, according to a controversial study.

It immediately drew angry denials from gay rights groups, and criticism from other scientists over the way it was conducted.

Its conclusion clashes with that of major mental health organisations, which say sexual orientation is fixed from birth and that so-called reparative therapy may be harmful.

Dr Robert L. Spitzer, a psychiatry professor at Columbia University in New York who led the study, said he cannot estimate what percentage of highly-motivated gay people can change their sexual orientation.

But he claims his research 'shows some people can change from gay to straight, and we ought to acknowledge that'.

He presented his findings yesterday at a meeting of the American Psychiatric Association in New Orleans and said he plans to submit his work to a psychiatric journal for publication. Critics of the study yesterday claimed that many of the 200 'ex-gays' who participated in the study were referred by religious groups which condemn homosexuality.

The issue has been hotly debated in the scientific community and among religious groups, some of which contend that gays can become heterosexuals through prayer and counselling.

Major mental health groups say nobody knows what causes a person's sexual orientation. Theories tracing homosexuality to troubled family dynamics or faulty psychological development have been discredited, the psychiatric association says.

Another body, the American Psychological Association, says most scientists think sexual orientation probably comes from a complex interaction, including biological and environmental factors.

Professor Spitzer spearheaded the psychiatric association's 1973 decision to remove homosexuality from its list of mental disorders, calling for more research to see whether some people can change sexuality.

Major mental health groups say nobody knows what causes a person's sexual orientation

For the new study, he conducted 45-minute phone interviews with 200 people, 143 of them men, who claimed they had changed from gay to heterosexual. The average age of those interviewed was 43.

They answered about 60 questions about their sexual feelings and behaviour before and after their efforts to change. Those efforts had started about 14 years before the interviews for the men and 12 years for the women.

Most said they had used more than one strategy to change their orientation. About half said the most helpful step was work with a mental health professional, most commonly a psychologist.

About one-third cited a support group, and fewer mentioned books and mentoring by a heterosexual.

Spitzer concluded that 66 per cent of the men and 44 per cent of the women had arrived at what he called good heterosexual functioning – a term whose definitions include being in a sustained, loving heterosexual relationship within the past year.

Psychologist Douglas Haldeman, of the University of Washington, who has evaluated reparative therapy, said there is no credible scientific evidence which suggests sexual orientation can be changed 'and this study doesn't prove that either'.

He said the participants appeared unusually skewed toward religious conservatives and people treated by therapists 'with a strong anti-gay bias'.

Michael King, professor of psychiatry at the Royal Free Hospital, London, said there were flaws in the way the study was conducted.

'There has never been any evidence that in the long term people actually change their sexual orientation,' he added. 'This would be an unusual finding, if true.

'But the only real way to see if these methods do affect sexual orientation is to have a randomised controlled study. Using telephone interviews with people who claim they have changed is not reliable evidence.'

• By Jenny Hope, Medical Correspondent

Homosexuality and the Church

Most Christians have believed and most churches have taught that you cannot be a Christian and express your love for another person of the same sex in a sexual relationship. They believe that God has condemned this through the Bible.

We must remind ourselves of the world the people of the Bible actually lived in. Life was hard, and survival was a nation's first concern. Today, in the West, we may find it hard to comprehend the emphasis placed on child-bearing in ancient societies. In biblical times people were faced every day with basic threats to their individual and communal survival. Therefore, forms of sexuality which seemed to be at odds with the institution of the family were rejected and condemned. The law of the Jews in Christ's time illustrated this general pattern, though in other respects it represented for its day a more careful and merciful code than the traditions of neighbouring peoples.

Christianity began as a Jewish sect; Christ was a Jew and so were all his apostles. Though the new Christian faith replaced the old Jewish law in the eyes of the early Christians, both are intimately and inextricably linked. Ancient fears about homosexuality were deeply founded in the consciousness of early Christians, whether Jewish or not, and Christianity itself certainly did not remove them.

The story of Sodom and Gomorrah is often quoted; but the real point of it is an understandable condemnation of what amounts to gang rape. It is not a condemnation of homosexual relationships as we would understand them today. It is significant that when Jesus used the story of Sodom he said that the people of that city would find the Day of Judgement easier to bear than those who refused to welcome his disciples and give them hospitality (Luke

LESBIAN ⊕ GAY CHRISTIANS

10:11-12). And whenever else the destruction of Sodom and Gomorrah is referred to in the Bible, homosexuality isn't even mentioned.

Jesus himself said nothing about homosexuality as such, but he did teach the importance of love and commitment in relationships. He condemned the Pharisees for keeping only to the letter of the law and for ignoring the fact that the law served a higher purpose. The Sabbath, like all of God's gifts to us, was made for us to use – with responsibility. And our sexuality is one such gift.

Paul in his letters condemned the practice of heterosexual men having intercourse with male prostitutes in pagan temples. He thought this idolatrous because human beings were used as objects of worship rather than honour being given to God. It was all destructive of love, and Paul then showed how Christ's power can rescue us from such a pattern of life if we commit ourselves to him in trust. God wants us, through Jesus, to love one another as he loved us (John 13:34).

In many respects the Church was limited by the social outlook of the times and places where the Gospel was preached. Attitudes have always changed, however slowly. Only in the last century was slavery abolished, but Paul accepted it without question. And it is only in recent times that the churches have started to examine the position of women in their own organisations and in society in general. The time is now right to have a critical look at homosexuality in a Christian context.

The Lesbian & Gay Christian Movement is not selling out on Christian truth. It is working for the very love and freedom that Christ brings to his people through his life, death and resurrection. Our Movement is working for love, for peace, for justice, and for the promotion of the Christian faith. God's work is always a struggle. Let us try to be at the heart of it.

• The above information is from the Lesbian & Gay Christian Movement's web site which can be found at www.lgcm.org.uk

Alternatively see page 41 for address details.

© Lesbian & Gay Christian Movement

-HE DIDN'T MENTION HOMOSEXUALITY...

...JUST WENT ON ABOUT LOVE...

Lesbians, gay men, bisexuals and mental health

Information from MIND

Bisexuality

Bisexual people face a number of pressures within society. Gay and lesbian communities may perceive of them as people who 'pass' or deny their real sexual identity to avoid the stigma of being gay or lesbian.[1] Heterosexual people may also view them as less than 'normal' or as inferior to heterosexuals, subjecting them to much the same homophobia faced by lesbians and gay men.[2] Bisexual women and men may also face pressure to 'make up their minds' and define themselves as either gay, lesbian or heterosexual. Some heterosexuals, and some lesbians and gay men, believe that bisexual people should declare their loyalty by choosing one exclusive sexual orientation.

In the 1980s bisexual women and men were largely ignored within most political debates amongst lesbians and gay men. Although change has been slow and there is still a long way to go, bisexuality is now being recognised and included by an increasing number of lesbian and gay groups and organisations. Bisexual people have begun to set up their own social and support groups and more is being written about bisexual women and men living in Britain today.

Lesbian, gay and bisexual youth

Lesbian, gay and bisexual youth are especially vulnerable to problems. The reasons for this are complex and interrelated. Gay youth face particular problems accepting themselves: they have often internalised a negative self-image and have not received accurate information about sexuality at a time when they most need it. They have even less knowledge about gay, lesbian and bisexual identities that is not pejorative. The young person may be told that they are 'acting out' or 'going through a phase'.

Young people need the support of family, friends and peers and so may try to conceal their sexual orientation to avoid the possibility of rejection. Adolescents generally have rigid attitudes and can be intolerant of differences in themselves and others; conformity to the group is important. Young people who identify themselves as lesbian, gay or bisexual have been found to be more susceptible to bullying at school. This has a variety of effects on academic performance and future mental health.

Ian Rivers of the University of Luton has conducted research into bullying and its subsequent effects on the mental health of gay and lesbian youth. One hundred and ninety lesbians, gay men and bisexual men and women participated in this research. Findings revealed that the bullying which lesbians and gay men experienced in school was more severe in nature than general bullying. 53 per cent of participants said that they had contemplated self-harm as a result of being bullied. 40 per cent indicated that they had attempted self-harm or suicide on at least one occasion. Of these three-quarters had attempted on more than one occasion.[3] In later life some of those bullied said that they experienced nightmares or flashbacks related to the bullying. Others said that they tended to avoid social situations or large gatherings for fear of experiencing a panic attack.[4]

Jan Bridget of the Lesbian Information Service has summarised the main points relating to lesbian and gay youth suicide. Her review of British and American research reveals that there are consistently higher figures for attempted suicide among young lesbians and gay men; that lesbian and gay youth are 2-6 times more likely to attempt suicide than heterosexual youth, and that the highest rates of suicide are among those who are isolated from support.

Black lesbians, bisexual women and men and gay men

Black people are so often stereotyped by the media as 'criminals' or 'sex-mad deviants' that the impression has stayed in the minds of many people. Similar myths are spread about gay people, for example, that lesbians hate men and that gay men assault little boys.

Black lesbians and gay men face double oppression because of their race and their sexuality. Some feel they have been forced to choose between the gay 'culture' and the Black and ethnic minority culture. Black communities can be homophobic, in the same ways white ones can be, but there is no evidence to suggest Black people are more homophobic. This is a racist myth based on misinformation.

Anne Hayfield (1995) makes the point that when homophobia occurs within Black communities this can mean that an individual is cut off from support networks of family and friends which are important to enable a person to develop a positive Black identity and to counter the racism faced on a daily basis. Black lesbians and gay men therefore have to consider the importance of 'coming out', weighing the possible loss of family and community support against the gains.[5]

Black lesbians, gay men and bisexual women and men also face discrimination from organisations that exist to support them. It seems that Black issues are often ignored within political/campaigning groups and in social/support groups and out on the 'scene'. Anne Hayfield claims that Black lesbians have often been refused admission to lesbian spaces and have been subjected to racism from white lesbians.[6]

Quibilah Montsho, a Black lesbian poet and survivor who was wrongly diagnosed as mentally ill and forced into hospital against her will, believes that as many as 60% of Black lesbians in this country have had, or will have, some experience of the mental health system during their lifetime. She describes psychiatry as both racist and homophobic, saying that what is classed as mental illness is defined and controlled by white straight men – inventing new forms of mental illness, diagnosis and treatments, all of which reinforce the racist concept that Black people are more prone to mental illness. She says that it is impossible for a Black lesbian to complain of sexism, racism and/or homophobia in a psychiatric setting because complaining may be interpreted as displaying an aspect of paranoid psychosis. This psychosis is seen to be suppressible either by increasing the dosage of medication or prescribing additional drugs. This means that it is unlikely that a Black person will feel safe to 'come out' to anyone within the mental health services. Quibilah also makes the point that because of language and cultural differences the service user/survivor can be misunderstood and further labelled as defensive or uncommunicative.[7]

Lesbians, gay men and bisexual women and men with disabilities

Lesbians, gay men and bisexual women and men with disabilities, like all people with disabilities, are not expected to have any sexuality at all, let alone an attraction to people of the same sex. Disabled people have generally been pressurised to play down their sexuality, both in wider society and in residential settings. Where the issue of sexuality is raised, most people with disabilities are assumed to be heterosexual.

Of course, the gay community is also affected by the ableism that exists in society generally. Gay people are also responsible for sometimes regarding people with disabilities as asexual and genderless. Gay, lesbian and bisexual events and venues are often difficult to access for people with disabilities.

Some lesbians, gay men and bisexuals may be dependent on heterosexual carers; this makes the process of 'coming out' risky. Some individuals rely on vital support networks and may be afraid of losing this support because of homophobia. This places considerable pressures on the individual.

Residential care, housing projects, etc. for people with disabilities are generally mixed-sex and geared towards heterosexuals. This is because of attitudes which deny an individual a right to a sexuality, whatever this may be. Even within the 'disability communities' lesbians, gay men and bisexuals with disabilities are often not accepted because they do not fit into heterosexist stereotyping.

Older lesbians, gay men and bisexual women and men

The term 'older' actually embraces a number of different generations. Some people like to identify themselves as 'older' and others do not. The issues for a forty-year-old lesbian or gay man are likely to be different from those relevant to a person of eighty. In this way, rigid categorisation can be disempowering and unhelpful.

Some older lesbians and gay men may have been subjected to psychiatric treatment in an attempt to 'cure' them. This may have left them with a legacy of guilt and potential emotional damage. Many others will have stayed 'closeted' throughout their lives. Others were active with

the Gay Liberation Movement and the Women's Movement; enabling more lesbians and gay men to find a safe place within society.

Ageism within society has meant that older people are generally seen as unattractive and socially boring. The 'gay scene' is no exception and is more often than not geared towards younger people. Despite the lack of social opportunities generally, some older lesbians and gay men have long-established support networks stretching back over many years. Others will be more isolated, perhaps due to the deaths of partners and friends, lack of mobility, or simply because they have lost touch with others.

Some organisations working with older people fail to take into account the fact that a service user may not be heterosexual. Sheltered housing and residential care is usually mixed-sex and geared towards heterosexuals. Some older lesbians and gay men get together to discuss alternatives to mixed-sex residential care or sheltered housing.

References
1 Garnets, L., Kimmel, D. (1991) Lesbian and Gay Male Dimensions in the Psychological Study of Human Diversity. In: Goodchilds (ed) *Psychological Perspectives on Human Diversity in America: Master Lectures.* pp.143-192. Washington DC. American Psychological Association.
2 Ibid.
3 Rivers, Ian (1997) *The long-term impact of peer victimisation in adolescence upon the well-being of lesbian, gay and bisexual adults.* Paper presented at the Psychological Society of Ireland's Annual Conference, Ireland, 13-15 November 1997.
4 Rivers, Ian (1997) Violence Against Lesbian and Gay Youth and its Impact, pp. 31-48. *Pride and Prejudice, working with lesbian, gay and bisexual youth,* Ed. Margaret S. Schneider, Central Toronto Youth Services.
5 Hayfield, Ann (1995) Several Faces of Discrimination. *Talking Black: Lesbians of African and Asian Descent Speak Out.* Cassell, pp. 186-206.
6 Ibid.

• The above information is from MIND's *Lesbians, gay men, bisexuals and mental health* factsheet from their web site at www.mind.org.uk
© MIND

Identity and sexuality

Information from the Maranatha Community

Introduction

Human relationships are at the core of civilised society.

Strong and permanent relationships based on mutual trust, respect and love undoubtedly strengthen society. Relationships which are temporary, shallow, debased and exploitative clearly weaken society. Relationships in which there is indifference and detachment are not neutral, they can be positively destructive.

The breakdown of relationships is a characteristic of contemporary society and with the obvious breakdown of marriage and the destruction of so many family units the issue of sexual relationships is increasingly the subject of public debate. Simultaneously with changes in legislation, the consequent alteration in behaviour patterns and the emergence of the AIDS crisis have also placed the issue of homosexual relationships in the arena of public discussion. This has undoubtedly caused much pain and deep divisions whilst partisan protagonists seek to normalise what others regard as abnormal behaviour. Much of the debate has sadly been driven by aggressive 'gay' pressure groups which have considerable public influence to obtain both platforms and funds for their movement. Their activities frequently involve coercion, threat and occasionally violence although doubtless the vast majority of homosexuals, being ignorant of these activities, would themselves disapprove of this behaviour.

On the other hand, however, it can be argued that many homosexuals, lonely and unhappy, have felt vulnerable and rejected. The emergence of a strident gay subculture often driven by commercial and political interests has tended to create exclusively gay ghettos and thus to separate homosexuals from the rest of the community. It has tended to divert attention away from the need for an understanding, caring

the maranatha community

and loving approach to the whole issue of male or female homosexuality.

What is homosexuality?

Homosexuality is essentially a confused condition and therefore there is confusion in its definition. Lawrence J. Hatterer in his book *Changing Homosexuality in the Male* defines the homosexual person as 'one who is motivated, in adult life by definite erotic attraction to members of the same sex and who usually, but not necessarily, engages in overt sexual relations with them'. To have a predisposition or propensity for members of one's own sex may not be a permanent situation. J. J. West in *Homosexuality Re-examined* (Duckworth 1977) stated, 'Few people pass through life without at some stage experiencing homosexual feelings'. He emphasised, 'Like other aspects of human behaviour, sexual orientation is the outcome of a complex interplay of different factors.' He pointed to these being mostly environmental, including general cultural habits and expectations, family upbringing and personal circumstances.

In one sense the homosexual through his or her orientation is expressing a profound psychological need or deficiency. Hence, according to Dr Elizabeth Moberley, to stop 'being a homosexual' means 'to stop being a person with same sex psychological deficits'.

Our starting point in considering homosexuality therefore must surely be that God does not put labels on anyone. All human nature is wounded and in need of healing and the one who is called 'a homosexual' must primarily be seen as a human being to be loved and treated with the same respect as any other person. The fact that one aspect of their life differs from the norm must never be an excuse for them being robbed of their dignity, worth and uniqueness.

Christians believe that every man and woman is created in the image of God. In spite of weaknesses and problems we are each of inestimable value in His sight. We believe that our relationships with each other are of immediate concern to God. They are directly influenced by the nature of our relationship with Him.

The current debate about homosexuality must be seen in the context of the rapid growth of promiscuity, the devaluation of marriage and in the encouragement of child sex instanced in the distribution of condoms to young schoolchildren.

Driven by commercial interests which are ruthless and amoral we have become a sex-obsessed society with a totally unnatural emphasis upon the sex act, often in the context of violence, as distinct from normal, healthy, loving human relationships. Bruce Gyngell, Managing Director of Yorkshire/Tyne Tees Television, speaking to the Royal Television Society, asked, 'What are we doing to our sensibilities and moral values and, more important, those of our children when, day after day, we broadcast an unremitting diet of violence, extremes of sexuality and negative behaviour?' As these commercial interests have become stronger they have become more greedy and have not hesitated to debase, degrade and devalue the relationships which should be valued for their gentleness, dignity and modesty. Children, in particular, have had ugly and sometimes frightening sexual images imposed upon them by irresponsible adults. The so-called 'National Condom Week' Report boldly proclaimed 'serial monogamy is the buzz phrase for the 1990s' and there is no doubt that there are now heavy pressures militating against life-long partnership in marriage. These pressures are of course generating immense human suffering, particularly amongst children.

Jesus comes to put right our relationships with God, with ourselves and with others. He specifically says, 'Whatever you did for the least of these brothers of mine, you did for Me' (Matt. 25.40).

A judgmental attitude can be deeply wounding and highly offensive, but on the other hand, a desire for good relationships should not blind us to the truth. In the emotionally charged debate on homosexuality which is currently taking place both in society at large and in the Church there is all too often a readiness to compromise the truth in order to be politically correct.

The first truth emphasised is that the incidence of homosexuality is far lower than we are led to believe. In the US Government General Social Survey of 1989, Professor Tom Smith of the University of Chicago undertook a survey of sexual behaviour. This showed that 98.5% of adults were exclusively heterosexual. Studies carried out in other countries show a remarkable consistency. A survey in the United Kingdom sponsored by the Wellcome Trust reported 1.4% of males having had a homosexual partner in the previous five years and 1.1% in the previous year. The Report claimed that the results were 'consistent with those from other recent studies in Europe and the United States'.

The second truth emphasised is that a high proportion of homo-

sexuals are deeply unhappy in their condition and would wish to change. In the 1992 SIGMA study funded by the Medical Research Council and the Department of Health no fewer than 34% of homosexual men expressed regret at being homosexual. Possibly more than this proportion felt regret but did not express it. 17% 'had considered giving up being gay' and 9% 'would take a pill today to make them heterosexual (if one were available)'. Recognition of this is important in really meeting the needs of those who are caught up in the 'gay' scene.

Homosexuality is essentially a confused condition and therefore there is confusion in its definition

---

Homosexual practice for many participants creates in its own right a stress level which makes the homosexual hypersensitive to criticism and to competition. Therefore, homosexual relationships are fraught with jealousies and angers and these are made worse by the promiscuous practice of multi-partnering. For the Christian the sex act is sacred and not to be taken lightly. Yet, sadly for many male homosexuals the physical sexual encounter is ephemeral as a result of encounters while 'cruising'. This in itself is a devaluation of relationships and inevitably has a high exploitative content. Love is about giving and receiving, not taking and dominating.

Promiscuity and multi-partnering robs the participant of their human dignity and debases sexuality. During the last century we have seen countless examples of the way in which the value of individual men and women has been swept on one side. Privacy has been invaded. Modesty, a fundamental ingredient in civilised society, has been ridiculed. The gentleness and beauty of sexual relationships in marriage have been scorned and torn apart. The process of dehumanisation has continued apace assisted by the media and militant secular humanist influences. We, by omission and apathy, encourage our children to have sex. Moreover, we teach them about sexuality without any real guidance on spiritual and moral factors, frequently imposing upon them the dogmas and doctrines of a very bigoted and intolerant humanistic minority.

The background

The predisposing factors and circumstances which may give rise to homosexuality are complex and numerous. The current debate about homosexuality centres largely upon basically whether it is genetic or acquired. If it is the former there ought to be considerable evidence available to show that it is genetic and/or organically determined. This evidence does not exist. As Lawrence Hatterer, the American psychiatrist, states, 'homosexuals are not born but made and genetic, hereditary, constitutional, glandular or hormonal factors have no significance in causing homosexuality' (Quoted in *The Church and Homosexuality* – Green, Holloway, Watson).

Dr Frank Lake, who pioneered clinical theology, discovered considerable evidence of the significance of disorders in infant years being directly related to the homosexual condition. All 50 male homosexual patients to whom Lake and his colleagues administered LSD between 1950 and 1966 relived a traumatic incident or painful period of babyhood in which life in the woman's care had been horrific. (quoted in *Christian Attitudes to Homosexuality* by Peter Coleman, pub. SPCK).

Doctor Charles W. Socarides of the Albert Einstein College of Medicine in New York states that homosexuality is not innate, it is learned, acquired behaviour. Even Masters and Johnson in their book *Human Sexuality* have written 'the genetic theory of homosexuality has generally been discarded today'. Dr John Money of the Johns Hopkins School of Medicine and Director of the Psychohormonal Research Unit states, 'Whatever may be the possible unlearned assistance from constitutional sources, the child's psychosexual identity is not written, unlearned in the genetic code, the hormonal system or the nervous system at birth.'

There is a remarkably high success rate in leading homosexuals into heterosexuality through Christian healing. Countless examples of this are to be found in the ministry of Leanne Payne. Rev. John Hampsch has given much evidence of the healing of homosexuals through the work of 'Desert Stream', one of twenty-five groups listed in the central referral agency of Exodus International. The way in which we perceive ourselves and others is fundamentally changed when a person grows in Christian faith.

There is a remarkably high success rate in leading homosexuals into heterosexuality through Christian healing

---

All the evidence points to the fact that homosexual orientation in adult life is the result of pre-birth and early childhood experiences.

As Doctor Elizabeth Moberley states, 'from the present evidence it would seem clear that the homosexual condition does not involve abnormal needs, but normal needs, that have abnormally, been left unmet in the ordinary process of growth. The needs as such are normal; their lack of fulfilment and the barrier to their fulfilment is abnormal.'

• The above information is an extract from *Healing Wholeness & Homosexuality*, produced by the Maranatha Community. See page 41 for their address details.

© The Maranatha Community

What is the gay gene?

Information from Stonewall

The term 'gay gene' refers to the gene that is thought to determine one's sexuality. Whether this gene actually exists is still subject to scientific debate.

Several studies have found there to be a genetic influence on the determining of one's sexuality – whether it be the levels of one's hormones or the size of certain parts of the brain (i.e., the corpus callosum or medulla oblongata). However, there is no conclusive proof that homosexuality is completely determined by genetic factors.

Eye colour, for example, is determined 100 per cent by genetic factors, but height is only 90 per cent determinable and is influenced by other factors such as nutrition. Because of this, height is said to be a 'multi-factorial' trait. Studies of monozygotic (identical) twins revealed that if one brother is gay, there is a 52 per cent chance that his twin is gay, suggesting a 70 per cent

attributable genetic factor (Bailey and Pillard, *A Genetic Story of Male Sexual Orientation*, 1990).

In the absence of conclusive proof as to whether homosexuality is completely biologically determined, the best answer is that the most current

---

Several studies have found there to be a genetic influence on the determining of one's sexuality – whether it be the levels of one's hormones or the size of certain parts of the brain

---

scientific studies suggest it to be a combination of environmental and biological factors. John Money, Emeritus Professor of Paediatrics at John Hopkins University, Maryland, USA, summarises the current scientific crux: 'Homosexuality is multi-varied. There is certainly a genetic component but there is not enough data to state that it is an exclusive influence. Hormones that affect the foetus play a part' ('Could You Be Gay for a Day?', *Daily Express*, 7 July 1996).

Even though popular medical opinion is not certain of the exact role that genetic factors play in determining one's sexual orientation, it is certain that homosexuality is not a disorder of any kind and should not be treated as such.

• The above information is from Stonewall's web site which can be found at www.stonewall.org.uk Alternatively, see page 41 for Stonewall's address details.

© Stonewall

Press for Change

Christine Burns explains why being a trans person is as 'natural' as being 'a bit of a genius' and then how a divorce case in 1970 took away their rights to everything that others take for granted

What's it all about?

Press for Change is a political lobbying and educational organisation, which campaigns to achieve equal civil rights and liberties for all transsexual and transgendered people in the United Kingdom, through legislation and social change.

That's what it says on our web index page, and on all of Press for Change's literature. But what, first of all, is a transgendered (or 'trans') person? And what are the tangible examples in their lives which lead to a claim for an inequality to be righted?

If you are one of the many people who think that trans people's interests start and stop with wanting to get married and correct their birth certificates for a little bit of privacy, then be prepared for a shock . . . and for a long and upsetting read.

What (or more politely who?) is a 'trans person'?

Labels are always hopelessly inadequate to describe the sheer diversity of human existence, and no more so in the area of sex and gender, where the most fundamental mistake of all is to assume that life is 'normally' simple and clear cut.

We're all taught that there are only two sexes, right? And people are born one sex or the other, right?

Wrong. Think about other human characteristics for a moment . . .

Are you a tall or a short? Are you a fat or a thin? A clever or a dim? A white or a black? A nice or a nasty?

Sometimes we use these simple distinctions, of course, but few would deny that they mask many shades and subtleties in every case. It is nature's design to encourage diversity, in order to maximise the chances of a species' survival . . . and so, on every plane of measurement you care to examine, people are seldom actually at one extreme or the other.

Most of us think of ourselves as 'average', which is a way of expressing the simple fact that we may be *generally* like the next person, but that doesn't mean we are identical. In fact, the combination of where we are on all the scales of measurement taken together . . . height, build, intelligence, skin colour, personality and all the rest . . . is what makes each of us absolutely unique.

So why should we be so naïve as to build a society on the peculiar assumption that sex . . . and the perception of which sex we are (our 'gender identity') should be simply one thing or another? We even know that people have different sized and shaped genitals, yet we're taught from our earliest recollections to assume that there is an exact cut-off point somewhere . . . or perhaps, more comfortably, a yawning unbridgeable chasm . . . on one side of which there are males, and on the other side of which there are females.

Ponder a statistic: one in every two hundred children born anywhere in the world has something which is a bit ambiguous about the most obvious physical manifestation of their sex . . . their external genitals. In about one in five of those cases (i.e. one in 1,000 babies) the ambiguity is sufficient that doctors may decide to take some sort of action to 'correct' the ambiguity. The quotes are significant, because thousands upon thousands of people grow up to vehemently resent that 'correction', carried out without their consent, depriving them of options which nature gave them, and very often destroying their capacity for sexual enjoyment.

We digress, perhaps . . . but the point is to illustrate that on a physical plane, there is no such thing as 'one sex or the other' . . . only a society constructed on the assumption that there is, and prepared to use surgery upon an otherwise healthy and comfortable child to maintain the myth by cutting away the evidence.

So it is with human personalities too, and the self-identificational part of ourselves which leads us to feel that we 'belong' with one sex or the other.

The *important* point is that there is no reason why the intangible bit (your identity) and the whole gamut of physical bits (your genitals, your internal reproductive organs and the chromosomes which first nudge a foetus in one direction or the other) need to develop in sync. The two are formed at very different times for one thing, and all have so much capacity for variation that they can easily vary in opposite directions and overlap.

For all sorts of reasons, therefore, people can find

that what they look like, how they feel, who they feel like, and how they'd like to be seen and treated by others brings them into conflict with the over-simplified contemporary norms of the society they live in.

When people live that conflict *openly*, by challenging the limitations upon their expression, we call them 'trans'. And, if you really *must* have further labels to try and break that down, transgendered people are those whose sense of self places them so far into the opposite camp to the one suggested by their physical sex characteristics, that they take varying steps to solve the conflict by altering or disguising those features. Again, simplistically, those who are happy enough to merely disguise their features using the powerful signals sent out by gendered clothing are dubbed 'transgendered' and those who go to the lengths of wishing to alter their physique to completely resemble the sex they feel themselves to belong to are labelled by medicine as 'transsexual'. Medicine 'owns' the transsexual label because, of course, transsexual people require the assistance of surgery to achieve a physical expression of who they are inside.

Usage of the terms differs, however, and has evolved over the years in line with a growing sophistication in trans people's own awareness. The above distinctions invite the assumption that 'transgendered' is in some way inferior or short of 'transsexual' for instance. More recently, therefore, the term 'transgender' has come to embrace both . . . and Press for Change and other organisations worldwide have gone a further step and now advocate the use of the adjective 'trans' to describe people who, in expressing their sense of identity, come into conflict with the contemporary gender behaviour norms of their society.

We stress however that whether you use the word 'trans' or older, more prescriptive, terms like 'transsexual' these are adjectives not nouns. It is no more polite to say that somebody is 'a transsexual' than 'he is a blind' or 'she is a deaf'. Please remember that trans people, transsexual people, transgender people . . .

. . . or whatever description you use . . . are people first, and the 'T' adjective describes only one of the many interesting and individual characteristics which make up that person.

So where does the discrimination come into this?

Now aren't you glad you asked?

The legal status of trans people in the UK is not actually defined by legislation, but generally determined by reference to the case law (jurisprudence) resulting from a now-infamous divorce case in 1970 (Corbett vs Corbett/Ashley – *All England Law Reports 1970* Vol 2 pp 32-51).

April Ashley, a model and transsexual woman, had married Arthur Corbett (the heir of Lord Rowallen) some two years previously. The marriage had not worked out and the Rowallen family was seeking a basis on which to end the marriage and yet avoid the inheritance issues which would normally be raised. Divorce law in Britain at that time required proof of adultery or cruelty; mutual consent was not admissible and, in any case, April did not wish to be divorced. Instead, therefore, a case was constructed on the premise that the marriage had never been legal in the first place (since she had been registered as a boy at birth) and should always therefore (and in perpetuity) be treated as male.

The case was contested quite strongly but medical opinion at the time was divided (the three experts on both sides disagreed about the etiology of transsexuality, and the manner in which the phenomenon should therefore be construed). Consequently the judge (Lord Justice

---

Medicine 'owns' the transsexual label because, of course, transsexual people require the assistance of surgery to achieve a physical expression of who they are inside

---

Ormrod), who was himself a medical man, felt obliged to construct a medical test and definition, by which the sex in such cases was to be determined. It is worth commenting at this point that the basis of his test would no longer be supported by any informed medical opinion, in the light of new knowledge in the intervening 30 years.

A significant precedent was thereby established, since up till that point no case law or legislative provisions for transsexual people was thought to have existed (although this belief is now questioned). Operated transsexual people simply applied and were allowed to have their birth certificate altered, and they then simply enjoyed the normal status accorded to citizens of their new sex. Desperate attempts were made at the time to try and limit the effect of the judgment to the issue of marriage but, in practice, as it remains the only judicial reference point in this matter, the outcome has been used as the basis on which to comprehensively deny this group of UK citizens the most basic of civil rights from the moment their treatment commences.

The consequences of the Corbett case

The practical consequences of the Corbett case over the last 30 years have extended to virtually every area of life for British trans people, to the extent that even Press for Change campaigners are not surprised to come across new implications or subtleties stemming from society's fundamental refusal to recognise the simple social reality of their existence in law. To try and do justice to the scope of what we campaign against, therefore, we have assembled, quite literally, an A to Z Encyclopaedic guide to the problems and indignities faced by . . . for all you know . . . the person sitting next to you now.

• The above information is an extract from Press for Change's web site which can be found at www.pfc.org.uk Alternatively see page 41 for their address details.

© Press for Change

Age of consent

Information from Stonewall

The age of consent is equal for all. In England, Wales and Scotland it is set at 16. In Northern Ireland it is 17. This change was brought about following the use of the Parliament Act in November 2000 following Stonewall's most successful campaign to date.

Does homosexual experience turn heterosexuals lesbian or gay?

Medical studies indicate that homosexual feelings are present before any kind of sexual encounter has taken place. This characteristic of homosexual behaviour was presented as early as 1957's Wolfenden Report, which stated that 'our medical witnesses were unanimously of a view that the main sexual pattern is laid down in the early years of life and the majority of them held that it was usually fixed in main outline by the age of sixteen. Many held that it was fixed much earlier.'

Forty years later, Project SIGMA also dispelled this oft-cited myth. According to this study of male homosexual behaviour in England and Wales which was funded by the Department of Health and the Medical Research Council, of the men in their study who had their first sexual experience after 15, 90% had already come to recognise their sexual 'difference'. Moreover, the majority of the young men in the study had their initial homosexual experience with young men of the same age (the study found that the average age difference between homosexual partners at their first sexual experience was just one year) (*Project SIGMA Position Paper on the Age of Consent*, 1994, p.1).

In addition, Project SIGMA found that the 'vast majority' of men 'hoped' and 'many actively sought'

their first homosexual encounter. Of the 1,100 men in the survey, the study did not find one participant who thought that his current sexual orientation was the result of seduction or other unwanted sexual activity at an early age.

The British Medical Association (BMA) agrees. It states that 'extensive research does not indicate that men aged 16-21 are in need of special protection because they may be recruited into homosexuality'. The BMA continued to state that 'evidence would suggest that reducing the age of consent to 16 would be unlikely to affect the number of men engaging in homosexual activity, either in general or within specific age groups' (*Age of Consent for Homosexual Men*, January 1994, p. 7).

What is the situation in other countries?

The table below lists the ages of consent for selected countries in Europe and the Commonwealth.

Age of consent

Country	Male/Female	Female/Female	Male/Male
Austria	16/14	14	18
Belgium	16/18	16/18	16/18
Canada	14/18	14/18	14/18
Cyprus	16	16	16
Denmark	15/18	15/18	15/18
England (UK)	16	16	16
Finland	16	16	16
France	15	15	15
Germany	16	16	16
Greece	15	15	15
Iceland	17	15	17
Ireland	16	16	16
Italy	14	14	14
Lithuania	16	16	18
Luxembourg	16	16	16
Malta	12/18	12/18	12/18
The Netherlands	12/16	12/16	12/16
New Zealand	16	16	16
Northern Ireland (UK)	17	17	17
Portugal	14	14	14
Romania	14	Illegal	Illegal
San Marino	14	14	14
Scotland (UK)	16	16	16
Spain	12/16	12/16	12/16
Sweden	15	15	15
Turkey	15/18	15/18	15/18
Wales (UK)	16	16	16

Where two ages are shown, this is either because a higher age applies where the older person is in a position of authority or influence over the younger, or because sexual activity is legal at the lower age unless the younger person subsequently complains.

What is the history behind the current age of consent?

Gay sex was decriminalised under the Sexual Offences Act 1967. At that time sex between two consenting males was legalised if those involved were aged 21 years or older. The age of consent for heterosexual sex was 16.

Twenty-one remained the age of consent for gay sex until the Criminal Justice and Public Order Act 1994, which lowered the age to 18. Although there was a push for equalising the age of consent at that time, 18 was accepted as a compromise under the guise that males developed sexually more slowly than females.

In May 1996 the European Court of Human Rights agreed to hear the case of Euan Sutherland v. United Kingdom which challenged the unequal age of consent. On 7 October 1997, the ECHR ruled that the unequal age of consent was unlawful, prompting the government to grant a free vote in the Commons regarding the matter.

On 22 June 1998 the House of Commons voted 336 to 129 to equalise the age of consent. On 22 July 1998 the House of Lords rejected 290-122 the amendment to the Crime and Disorders Bill 1998 which would have equalised the age of consent at 16.

On 25 January 1999 the House of Commons voted again, 313 to 130, to equalise the age of consent, this time part of the Sexual Offences Bill 1999. Not much later, the House of Lords threw out the Commons vote, meaning that the age of consent for gay males remains at 18.

On 30 November 2000 the Parliament Act was invoked and its provisions ensured that the Sexual Offences (Amendment) Bill was passed for Royal Assent. It is now law and we await a decision from the Home Office on a commencement date.

New battle for gay couples' rights

By Gaby Hinsliff, Chief Political Correspondent

Gay rights campaigners will throw down the gauntlet to Labour this week with a major campaign for legal recognition of same-sex partnerships. The move comes amid fears that Ministers have pushed the repeal of Section 28, which bans the promotion of homosexuality in schools, on to the backburner.

The new battleground will be over extending property, tax and other rights enjoyed by married couples to same-sex peers. Lifelong gay partners have fewer rights than distant cousins: there have been cases of partners losing their homes when their lover dies since they have no right to inherit property, or shut out of decisions over the treatment of seriously ill partners because they are not recognised as next of kin.

Liberal Democrats are ready to try to secure a change in the law through a private member's bill in the House of Lords. Although it is unlikely to succeed, the aim is to prod the Government into acting.

The novelist Jeanette Winterson, the Labour-supporting financier Ivan Massow and other well-known figures are backing the campaign, which is also supported by a coalition of gay pressure groups, including Stonewall. It will

begin next week with the launch of a website, www.gaypartners.org to canvass opinion.

Spokesman Mark Watson said partnership rights reform could be more acceptable to MPs and peers than the controversial battle over Section 28 and the age of consent. 'We are not talking about 16-year-olds having sex, or sex in schools, which everybody gets nervous about,' he said. 'This is about couples saying, 'We have been together 15 years and we don't have the rights that a heterosexual couple who got married yesterday take for granted.'

Church leaders oppose any move towards so-called 'gay marriage'. But Watson said the campaign would not necessarily push for legalised gay weddings, but for a legal framework in which partners enjoyed basic safeguards.

Section 28

Section 28 of the Local Government Act 1988 states that no local authority shall 'promote homosexuality' nor 'the acceptability of homosexuality as a pretended family relationship'.

A move by the Labour government to repeal section 28 as part of the Local Government Bill was defeated in the House of Lords by 270-228 votes at the end of July 2000.

What is section 28?

Section 28 is a throwback to a more intolerant age. It has no place in the new Britain

This is not a quotation from New Labour. It is how the *Sunday Times* described section 28 when it was passed in 1988.

Section 28 of the Local Government Act 1988 amends Section 2A of the Local Government Act 1986. It prohibits a local authority from intentionally promoting homosexuality, or publishing materials with the intention of promoting homosexuality. It also prohibits local authorities from teaching the acceptability of homosexuality as a 'pretended' family relationship in any maintained school.

What does section 28 mean?

The truthful answer is: who knows? 'Promote' has no precise meaning in law. Legal advice has suggested that action by local authorities to discourage discrimination against homosexuals, or providing advice and assistance to lesbians and gay men, does not constitute promotion of homosexuality, but there have been no test cases.

In relation to schools, the introduction of local management in schools has reduced the intended impact of the legislation. The section applies to local authorities, but not to teachers or governors. As legislation, section 28 is confusing and unclear. But its message – that lesbians and gay men are less acceptable in society – continues to haunt schools and local authorities.

What section 28 says

28. – (1) The following section shall be inserted after section 2 of the Local Government Act 1986 (prohibition of political publicity) –
2A (1) A local authority shall not –
a. intentionally promote homosexuality or publish material with the intention of promoting homosexuality;

b. promote the teaching in any maintained school of the acceptability of homosexuality as a pretended family relationship.

What does section 28 do?

Shortly after section 28 was passed, there was a wave of violent attacks on the lesbian and gay community. The offices of a gay newspaper, *Capital Gay*, were burnt down, and lesbian and gay helplines reported a threefold increase in queer bashing.

During the House of Commons debates on section 28, concerns were raised about the alarming increase in violence and harassment against lesbians and gay men. Mrs Kellet-Bowman MP, one of the key proponents of Clause 28 (as it was then known) indicated that such violence was 'quite right' and that she supported such activities because it demonstrated an 'intolerance of evil'.

Many local authorities either panicked, or used the law to punish what they perceived as an unpopular group.

Homophobic bullying in schools

Most serious, however, has been the effect of section 28 in schools and colleges, despite the fact that section 28 only applies to local authorities who are no longer responsible for the management of schools and colleges.

There is now considerable evidence that homophobic bullying and abuse is widespread in schools. A 1999 study on sexual bullying (Rivers, 'Social Exclusion, Absenteeism and Sexual Minority Youth', *Support for Learning*, vol. 15), the 1997 study carried out by the Institute of Education (*Playing It Safe*, Douglas, Warwick, Kemp and Whitty) and the 1996 national survey of hate crimes against lesbians and gay men conducted by Stonewall (*Queer Bashing*, Mason and Palmer) all point to worrying developments in the extent of bullying.

● The above information is an extract from Stonewall's information on section 28 which features on their web site. See their web site at www.stonewall.org.uk for further information. Alternatively, see page 41 for Stonewall's address details.

© *Stonewall*

Gay job protection soon

Courtesy of the European Union

An historic step for gay rights has been taken by European Union Ministers. They have ratified a Directive to outlaw discrimination against gay people by employers throughout the EU. The Directive seeks to ensure equal treatment and combat discrimination on the grounds of sexual orientation in employment and occupation. The Directive is number 565 and it covers pay, benefits and conditions, recruitment, promotion and dismissals. The TUC welcomed the move. Peter Purton, Lesbian and Gay Policy Officer of the Trades Union Council, said: 'In Britain, for the first time, the Government will now be obliged to end discrimination on grounds of sexual orientation.'

It is encouraging that none of the ministers opposed the basic principle of equality in employment for gays and lesbians when the Directive was agreed in Luxembourg on 17 October, 2000. By far the most contentious area of debate in the months leading up to the Directive's finalisation was the extent of exemptions to be afforded to religious organisations. These heated disagreements continued right up to the Council of Ministers' meeting, with the Irish reportedly threatening to veto the whole Directive unless religious organisations were given more freedom to discriminate. The procedure for agreeing the Directive was complex. The Employment and Social Affairs Committee issued a draft directive for discussion and then recommended a version for the European Parliament. British (New Labour) MEP Stephen Hughes had persuaded the Committee that every member state be required to give religious organisations wide exemptions. Then it was the turn of the European Parliament.

The European Parliament reversed this requirement in a closely fought vote. The vote was proposed

by Baroness Ludford MEP after detailed briefings from Britain's National Secular Society. The Parliament's decisions are subject to ratification by the Council of Ministers. They accepted that there should be no compulsion to give these exemptions but had to make further concessions after fierce pressure from Ireland and Germany. These were to allow member states, if they wished, to permit existing employment discrimination by religious organisations to continue. In the UK this will mean that church schools will retain the statutory right in many cases to refuse employment or to sack teachers who do not conform to a school's religious ethos. Our own Parliament must pass legislation to

---

'In Britain, for the first time, the Government will now be obliged to end discrimination on grounds of sexual orientation'

---

give effect to the Directive, and deadline for the sexuality provisions is October 2003. The UK had argued for a much longer implementation period, although this may have been because of Government concerns over aspects of the Directive unconnected with sexuality. It is already accepted by all parties that religious organisations will be able to discriminate (for example, in favour of believers and against gays) in the appointment of such posts as priests and rabbis. When the legislation is introduced, however, the Government will have to decide whether to grant any exemptions allowing religious organisations to discriminate further. Religious organisations, especially those in the care and welfare sectors, will be lobbying for the right to refuse employment to non-believers, or even gays – even if the jobs are paid out of the public purse. We can expect a torrent of such demands which will no doubt be supported by organisations such as the Christian Institute and the Evangelical Alliance. On the other hand, the National Secular Society, gay campaigning organisations, such as the Gay and Lesbian Humanist Association, and the trade unions will be fighting to oppose any exemptions granted to religious organisations by this legislation. How are these conflicting demands by such religious organisations to be reconciled with those of secularists and humanists, as well as the lesbian and gay community? We can expect a number of cases to be brought in UK courts resulting in precedents being established.

• This briefing is based on an article written by Keith Wood for the December 2000 issue of *Gay Times*.

As well as being a member of the Gay and Lesbian Humanist Association (GALHA), Keith is Executive

Director of the National Secular Society (NSS) which is the major campaigning organisation fighting for the rights of the non-religious, the elimination of religious privilege and the separation of Church and State.

• GALHA's e-mail address is secretary@galha.org and its website is www.galha.org

NSS's e-mail address is kpw@secularism.org.uk and its web site is www.secularism.org.uk

Discrimination against lesbian and gay employees

Information from Lesbian and Gay Employment Rights (LAGER)

General legal rights

Even though a lesbian or gay man may have no direct legal remedy for discrimination they may be able to use other employment rights to bring some form of claim.

Most of these legal claims will be argued under statutory rights, the principal ones referred to in this article being unfair dismissal and sex discrimination. These rights are often qualified so a claim for unfair dismissal requires an employee to have been in employment for one year.

Examples of general legal rights which can be used include such claims as negligence claims, unfair dismissal and a failure to pay wages. Taking the latter example, the failure to pay wages or the deduction from pay is actionable by a claim to an industrial tribunal. The reason for the failure to pay wages is irrelevant; only the contractual right to a wage needs to be proved. On the other hand a failure to promote an employee would not be actionable in most cases as an employer would be unlikely to give someone such a right in their contract of employment.

Unfair dismissal

The remedy of unfair dismissal is actionable only if employment has

ended. You cannot obtain an injunction to prevent dismissal; there is a limited right of an injunction to force an employer to adopt any contractual procedures to dismiss, this could extend employment until the earliest contractual date of termination.

The remedy of unfair dismissal and constructive dismissal is possible for employees who have been employed for one year or more.

Resigning from work and claiming constructive dismissal.

An employer owes duties to employees to support them at work when faced with discrimination etc. It is far from certain that harassment itself from fellow employees will be a justifiable reason to resign and claim constructive dismissal.

Constructive dismissal relies upon the employee resigning from employment as soon as it is apparent that there has been a 'fundamental breach of contract' by the employer. This is often a question of fact which sometimes can only be decided by a tribunal after the employee has resigned.

Often in harassment cases the employee doesn't resign immediately but may put up with the harassment or 'go off sick' either genuinely or as a means to avert further discrimination. A long delay returning to work can and often will defeat a claim of constructive dismissal. Constructive dismissal often requires an employee to resign as soon as it is clear that the employer has breached 'the contract of employment'.

When resigning from employment is not a legal option, the employee is of course at risk of being sacked, possibly legally, for their absence from work. One tactic is to make it explicit, to the employer, that absence is due to the employer's failure to take steps to make the workplace free of harassment and to request that steps are taken by the employer to make the work environment safe.

If the employer instead dismisses the employee, it is open to an employee to argue on the facts that while the dismissal was for absence it was not just and equitable to use this as a reason to dismiss.

If the harassment represents a serious danger to a person's health and safety, it could be argued that the dismissal was for a health and safety reason, which could be automatically unfair. However the latter argument is far from tested.

These arguments place a heavy burden on an employee to prove their case, but may give a remedy when a constructive dismissal claim won't.

Dismissal for a reason related to the employee being lesbian or gay

It is rare for employers to argue that they dismissed an employee simply because they were gay or lesbian. It is equally unlikely that a tribunal would uphold such a decision. If an employer is seeking to justify the dismissal of a lesbian or gay man it is more common to argue that a particular feature of their sexuality caused them to be unsuitable for their job. The most common arguments are that they were a risk to children or young people or in the case of gay men that they had a criminal conviction for a sexual offence.

Risk to children or young people

There is clear authority that if an employee is lesbian or gay and employed in a job where they are responsible or have access to young people or children, then it is legitimate to dismiss them if the employer believes that they are a sexual risk (*Saunders v. Scottish National Camps* (1980)).

The disturbing feature of *Saunders* is that, even if it can be shown that the employer's belief is mistaken at the tribunal, the employer's reason at the time of dismissal can still be upheld as fair. In terms of advisers dealing with cases involving teachers and social workers it is important to insist on fair hearings before any dismissal, then evidence on the issue can, at the least, be considered.

Criminal convictions for sexual offences

It is not uncommon for employers to discriminate or dismiss gay men who have been convicted of a sexual offence, committed outside work, of which there is no heterosexual equivalent. The principal consensual gay offence being gross indecency.

As a matter of law, it has been held fair for employers to dismiss employees for an offence of gross indecency, where the employer believed there to be evidence that a lecturer 'could not control himself in public' and should not be trusted with young persons. (*Gardiner v. Newport County Borough Council* (1974)).

The most common arguments are that they were a risk to children or young people or in the case of gay men that they had a criminal conviction for a sexual offence

---

The case is distinguishable on its facts as the employee was a teacher. Advisers who represent gay men ought to argue that there is no relation between the alleged or proven conviction for a 'gay offence' and their job. This is necessary in order to counter the type of prejudicial trust and confidence argument which will often be used by the employer.

Failure to reveal convictions

The Rehabilitation of Offenders Act 1974 provides protection for employees which may assist them if they have been convicted of a gay only offence but only if it is a spent conviction.

Advisers ought to be aware of the limitations of the Act. Certain employments are excluded – e.g. social workers who have contact with vulnerable adults or children. Meaning that such employees are required to reveal all convictions when requested to do so. Additionally, depending on the sentence received for the offence, the conviction may not have become spent. If this is the case, failing to disclose a conviction may not only be a fair reason to dismiss, it can also be a criminal offence (obtaining employment by deception) if, having been asked, they have not disclosed the conviction in the first place.

Alternatively if the conviction is spent, then a refusal to employ, or the dismissal of an employee for failing to disclose a spent conviction, will almost certainly be an unfair reason to dismiss.

Sex discrimination argument

It is arguable that dismissing a man because he has committed an offence which can only be committed by a man is either an act of direct or indirect sex discrimination.

This is by no means a straightforward argument. Advisers could either show that dismissing men for gender-based offences was direct discrimination. Or they could seek to show that the employer applied a condition to men and women, namely that they would not employ people convicted of (consensual sexual) offences and this had a disproportionate impact on men.

Harassment at work

The idea of suing an employer for harassment has been little explored and there are few reported cases. However there is a basis both in criminal and civil law to say that such behaviour is unlawful. There are potential remedies for harassment which occurs at work and/or from other employees. How this can be married with employment rights is difficult to predict.

Harassment as a criminal offence

Both the Criminal Justice and Public Order Act 1994 and the Protection of Harassment Act 1997 created several criminal offences of harassment. Neither of the laws need proof of the motive for the harassment.

Harassment has to be intentional but the 1997 Act defines intentional as including behaviour which someone ought to know (but is not necessarily proven to have known) would cause distress. Both laws cover workplace harassment and the 1997 Act would cover abusive telephone calls to someone's home.

Civil remedies

As a general rule there is no reason why an employer cannot be sued for injury caused to an employee at work. The law of health and safety and the law of negligence provide that an employer needs at the least to make the workplace as safe as reasonably practical. However an employer does have a defence if he was not informed of the harassment.

There is also another limitation to a negligence action – you have to prove injury. In many cases the person leaves work in fear of injury rather than because of it. Those who can show stress caused by the harassment may have a claim but

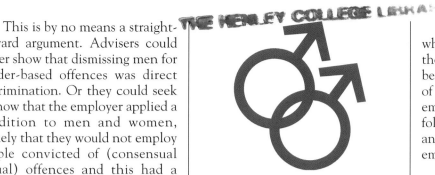

few fall within the level of psychiatric injury required by the law.

The 1997 Harassment Act seems to have now provided a more useful harassment remedy which is not dependent on proving injury before action can be taken. Indeed the 1997 Act also allows you to apply for an injunction.

Equal opportunities policies

The creation of a climate of equal opportunities or diversity at some workplaces has done more than the law to improve lesbian and gay employment rights. Nevertheless there is now legal authority that an Equal Opportunities Policy could be used to enhance the legal rights of employees.

The new anti-harassment laws should help lesbians and gays. They ought to strengthen the obligation on employers to offer support to people suffering both discrimination and harassment at work

---

A recent case called *Secretary of State for Scotland v. Taylor* (1997) held that an equal opportunities policy dealing with age discrimination was of legal effect and was not simply a mission statement. On the other hand in *Grant v. South-West Trains Ltd.* the judge found that an equal opportunities policy did not create legal rights to be protected from discrimination.

The cases can be understood on the factual basis that in *Taylor* it was clear that the Equal Opportunities Policy was incorporated into the employee's contract of employment: this was not the case in *Grant*.

There are a number of cases which LAGER has dealt with where the Equal Opportunities Policy has been referred to in a written contract of employment as binding on the employee. In these cases it would follow that it must therefore create an obligation of enforcement on the employer.

It remains to be seen what remedy, if any, the courts will provide when both the equal opportunities policy and the contract of employment are breached.

Conclusion

The new anti-harassment laws should help lesbians and gays. They ought to strengthen the obligation on employers to offer support to people suffering both discrimination and harassment at work. But if anything is clear about the anti-harassment laws so far, it is the fact that they haven't been used much! The only area where test cases may take place on the issue of sexuality is in the area of unfair dismissal law. But what is the right test-case to take?

With the possible exception of sexual harassment claims, sexuality discrimination claims can only be brought under the Sex Discrimination Act in cases where it is shown that lesbians were treated worse than gay men or vice versa. Some may say that this is no more than a right to complain of sex discrimination, whereas others may say it covers some element of sexuality discrimination. Who knows how this new test will apply in practice. Will employers find it difficult to show that they treat lesbians and gays equally badly? Will lesbians and gays find it easy to show that one is worse off than the other?

• While LAGER advises on individual cases, the views expressed in this article are not intended to be relied upon as legal advice in a particular case.

Also, one area that this article does not consider is any possible legal rights or remedies under the Human Rights Act. LAGER advisers are employment law specialists and the Human Rights Act falls outside of this remit.

© 2001 Lesbian and Gay Employment Rights (LAGER)

Be biased in favour of gays judges are told

Judges should make allowances for homosexuals to compensate for the prejudice they suffer in their daily lives, controversial courtroom guidance urged yesterday.

They should understand why some gays may be evasive in the witness box and accept their sexuality as an unalterable fact rather than a conscious choice.

Homosexuals and women are the victims of unfairness in the legal system, the guidelines insist, and judges must adjust their thinking in the cause of equality.

Victims of date rape can suffer worse than women raped by a stranger.

The recommendations prompted deep concern from family campaigners last night, and are bound to provoke a backlash both inside and outside the legal profession.

The guidance – in three new chapters of the *Equal Treatment Bench Book* issued by the Judicial Studies Board – will be sent to all judges.

The board is funded by Lord Chancellor Lord Irvine's Whitehall department and independently run by judges to 'provide training and instruction for all full-time and part-time judges in the skills necessary to a judge'.

Last year the first chapters of the Bench Book prompted controversy with advice that Rastafarians regard smoking cannabis as a religious sacrament.

This year's additions also suggest avoiding using a string of common expressions on the grounds that they show prejudice.

'Man and wife'; girl; workman and businessman are said to be unfair to women. When describing disabilities, the words 'handicapped' and 'mental illness' are to be avoided, judges are urged.

They are advised not to worry about any danger of undermining the institution of marriage if they grant new legal rights to homosexuals or 'alternative family forms'.

By Steve Doughty, Social Affairs Correspondent

'Families that do not strictly conform to the traditional model are an increasingly common social reality,' the guidelines say. The Lord Chancellor last night moved to distance himself from the new advice. Lord Irvine 'has not had an opportunity to study the latest Bench Book update', a spokesman said.

Judges are told to avoid offensive labels for homosexuality, unless they are used to expose someone's 'bigoted attitude'

But Colin Hart of the Christian Institute, which campaigned against lowering the homosexual age of consent to 16, said: 'This is malevolent and unbelievable. The section on homosexual equality could have been written by the Stonewall pressure group.'

Last night Sir David Keene, chairman of the Judicial Studies Board's equal treatment advisory committee, insisted: 'We are emphatically not telling judges what they should do or how they should exercise functions and, far less, tell them what they should do in any particular case.'

He said that judges sometimes needed help in understanding the modern world.

'We live in an increasingly complex society and it's difficult for someone to comprehend the background of a particular individual who appears before them in court,' he said.

On homosexuality

On homosexuality, judges are told: 'When dealing with apparent lack of candour, judges should remember that being gay or lesbian is an individual experience that may have led to fear and concealment.'

The guidance says that gays live in constant fear of unequal treatment. Homosexuality is not experienced as a choice but an unalterable fact.

As many as one in ten of the population are lesbian, gay or bisexual, the guidelines say, and as many as five million people in Britain have a 'minority sexual orientation'.

Although no accurate count of the homosexual population has yet been done, this advice conflicts with Government statistics indicating that no more than 400,000 men are of homosexual orientation and the highly respected Social Attitudes and Lifestyle analysis which in 1994 found that only one in 100 men had had homosexual sex in the past year.

The Bench Book says that sexual orientation is established before the age of puberty and adds: 'The vast majority of young gay men are aware of their sexual orientation before 16, and seek partners of about their own age.'

The advice says it is 'offensive' to link homosexuality with paedophilia.

Judges are told to avoid offensive labels for homosexuality, unless they are used to expose someone's 'bigoted attitude'.

On transvestites, the advice is that 'cross-dressing is not a fetish, but an inescapable emotional need, which, particularly in public places, generates risk of conflict or ridicule'.

On the family

The Human Rights Act will mean judges will have to consider whether European rules mean homosexual couples are entitled to be considered as fully legal families, the Bench Book says.

It dismisses the idea, held by a number of senior politicians in both major parties, that extending full legal rights to sexual minorities undermines the legal status of marriage for those who want to live in traditional families.

'This depends on acceptance of the proposition that to promote the rights of one category of citizen necessarily undermines those of another,' the guidance says. 'That argument would seem curious if applied to the rights of women versus men or to the rights of a racial minority versus the majority.

'Families that do not conform to the traditional ideal are an increasingly common social reality.'

It cites controversial research showing children brought up by homosexual parents do as well as those brought up by heterosexual couples in terms of well-being, sexual responsibility, academic achievement and avoiding crime.

Critics point to Australian research suggesting children of gay couples suffer disadvantage on a par with those of single parents.

Banned words

Judges should 'avoid words that imply an evaluation of the sexes', the guidelines state.

These include 'man and wife' – instead 'husband and wife' should be used. Girl is wrong unless applied to a child.

Occupational terms that apply to one sex are also out: instead of spokesman, judges should say representative.

Worker should be used instead of workman; and business people or executives rather than the term businessmen.

In dealing with disabled people, the phrase 'the disabled' should not be used. Handicapped should be banned and 'person with a disability' used instead. Rather than 'mental handicap' judges should say 'learning difficulties'. Instead of 'mental illness', they should say 'person with a mental health problem'.

'The blind' or 'the deaf' should become 'blind people' or 'people who are deaf', the Bench Book says.

Epileptic and arthritic should be 'person with epilepsy' or 'person with arthritis'.

Gay partners will get crime payouts

By Rebecca Paveley, Political Reporter

Gays and lesbians will be entitled to cash payouts if their partners die as a result of crime, it was announced yesterday.

Radical changes to the criminal compensation system, costing £20million, were unveiled in the House of Lords by Lord Bassam.

Until now, only parents, children, spouses or long-term heterosexual partners of those killed by crime could claim compensation because same-sex couples were not recognised by the Criminal Injuries Compensation Authority.

Gay rights campaigners had called for the law to be brought in line with that for heterosexual, non-married couples, who can claim if they have been together for more than two years.

The pressure has paid off and, under the reforms, homosexuals will get £10,000 if their partner dies – the same as heterosexuals.

If approved, the changes could come into force as early as April 1.

They were prompted by the three deaths in the bombing of the Admiral Duncan gay pub, in Soho by David Copeland.

Following the attack in 1999, Julian Dykes, whose wife Andrea was killed, was awarded £10,000. But Gary Partridge, whose partner John Light was also killed, received nothing.

The changes reinforce Home Secretary Jack Straw's pledge for compensation reform which he gave to Labour's spring conference at the weekend.

But Tory MP Gerald Howarth called the move a 'further step in the Government's relentless assault on marriage'.

'At this rate, it won't be long before the Government accedes to demands for homosexual marriages,' he said.

'Marriage is being completely downgraded by Labour – they are taking away all incentives for couples to marry.

'The battle is on to try and preserve the family, which study after study has shown is best for happiness, and best for children.'

Mr Straw has also pledged to increase other payouts following outrage over the compensation to nursery nurse Lisa Potts after she was injured while shielding children from a machete-wielding maniac.

She was given just £1,000 for the horrific injuries she suffered, in a total award of £49,000, which included cash for psychological scars.

Under the new proposals, minimum awards for rape victims will rise by nearly 50 per cent, from £7,500 to £11,000. Awards for serious multiple injuries will also increase. The current formula gives 100 per cent of the tariff for the most serious injury, ten per cent for the second and five per cent for the third.

It will be changed to 100 per cent, 30 per cent and 15 per cent.

There will also be ten per cent increases to awards for injuries such as severe head burns, which will increase to £16,500, repeated sexual abuse of children – where the award will go up to £8,200 – and loss of a hand or arm, where the victim would now get £44,000.

But victims with other injuries will not get increased compensation. For example, the level for a broken nose will stay at £1,000 and that for severe brain damage will remain at the maximum, £250,000.

Additional payments will also be given to victims criminally infected with HIV and Aids.

Gay marriages

Gay marriages may have to be made legal, says top judge

Parliament will be compelled by the Human Rights Act to consider legalising homosexual marriage, England's most senior family judge said last night.

Dame Elizabeth Butler-Sloss said the Act might overthrow the law that says marriage is a union between a man and a woman.

'I don't know how long that will remain the position,' she said.

'I suspect that within a comparatively short time, Parliament will have to grapple with the concept of same-sex marriage, divorce and post-divorce rights.'

Home Secretary Jack Straw suggested last month that gay marriage might be on the cards and that MPs could be allowed a free vote – a suggestion he later withdrew.

But Dame Elizabeth, president of the High Court family division, said last night: 'I imagine that Parliament will have a free vote.'

She said the legal route to homosexual marriage would be through a co-habitation law that would give right of kin to live-in couples, whether they were heterosexual or gay.

'My guess is we are a long way from same-sex marriage as such,' the judge said. 'We are a short way from Parliament giving some rights to those who have same-sex relationships.'

In a lecture to the Mothers' Union she said she could not predict the full impact of the Human Rights Act. But in the 21st century, rights for people in same-sex unions was something people would have to come to terms with.

'The most likely thing is that Parliament will be asked to provide something short of marriage by way of provision for those who are not married,' she said.

'There is a great discussion at the moment that men and women who co-habit are done down because they do not have the same rights as married couples.

'That is something that society will have to come to terms with as it is expressed within Parliament.'

Dame Elizabeth repeated her opinion – first given last year – that the law should allow homosexual couples to adopt children.

'We have got to live with the reality of the 21st century. In striving for what is best, we cannot dismiss what is good in other relationships'

She added that it was necessary to recognise that families existed in many forms and successful families were not limited to those headed by married couples.

'We have got to live with the reality of the 21st century,' she said. 'In striving for what is best, we cannot dismiss what is good in other relationships.'

She also confirmed that plans for no-fault divorce are now effectively dead. Lord Chancellor Lord Irvine has shelved part two of the Family Law Act passed by MPs more than four years ago but never put into practice. Dame Elizabeth said: 'There are major problems about its implementation from a procedural and practical point of view. It has major logistical problems in ever being implemented.'

Her prediction of a law for co-habiting and same-sex couples comes as Lord Irvine prepares to consider the idea this winter.

His officials have indicated that he finds the present law that gives few rights to unmarried couples 'unsatisfactory' and the Government's law reform quango, the Law Commission, is to deliver a report soon.

Dame Elizabeth's remarks indicate that she expects a challenge to be brought under the Human Rights Act that will call for clauses in the European Convention on Human Rights protecting the right to family life to be applied to gay and unmarried couples as much as to married people. The Act brings the Convention into British law.

She is the second senior member of the judiciary in a week to warn of far-reaching upheavals because of the Act.

Last week Lord Chief Justice Lord Woolf said it could lead to the freeing of Moors murderer Myra Hindley.

• By Steve Doughty, Social Affairs Correspondent

Laws relating to young LGBs

Information from the Peer Support Project

The age of consent

On Thursday 30 November 2000 the age of consent for gay men was brought in line with the age of consent for everyone else. It also introduced a statutory age of consent for lesbian sex. The age of consent, for everyone, is now 16 in England, Wales and Scotland, and 17 in Northern Ireland.

The Sexual Offences (Amendment) Act also deals with 'abuse of trust'. This means that it is illegal for someone in a position of trust (e.g. a teacher or youth worker) to have a sexual relationship with someone aged between 16 and 18.

Also, an underage person is no longer committing an offence if they have gay sex with someone over the age of consent. (The older person is, of course.)

'Gross indecency'

Straight sex is basically legal except where specifically prohibited (e.g. in public). However gay sex is basically illegal except where specifically permitted. This is because of an 1885 (Victorian) law that created the offence of 'gross indecency' that prohibits consenting sexual contact between men. (Non-consenting sex between men is treated as sexual assault or male rape.) The offence of gross indecency is still with us today because the Sexual Offences Act of 1967 only partially decriminalised gay sex, making it legal only if in private where no more than two people are present.

The Home Office is currently carrying out a major review of our outdated and rather silly sex laws, including gross indecency.

Section 28 – homosexuality in schools

Section 28 was a piece of legislation introduced by Thatcher's Conservative government, supposedly written to 'protect' young people. However it is a bigots' charter.

Specifically, Section 28 states: 28 – (1) The following section shall be inserted after section 2 of the Local Government Act 1986 (prohibition of political publicity) – 2A – (1) A local authority shall not:

a) intentionally promote homosexuality or publish material with the intention of promoting homosexuality

b) promote the teaching in any maintained school of the acceptability of homosexuality as a pretended family relationship.

(2) Nothing in subsection (1) above shall be taken to prohibit the doing of anything for the purpose of treating or preventing the spread of disease.

(3) In any proceedings in connection with the application of this section a court shall draw such inferences as to the intention of the local authority as may

---

Ignorance and homophobic bullying frequently go unchallenged, and young LGBs in schools do not get the support they deserve

---

reasonably be drawn from the evidence before it.

Whether by accident or design Section 28 is totally unworkable. What, for example, is promoting homosexuality? Buy one get one free? Hmm. Therefore no one has ever been prosecuted under Section 28. Even so, a survey conducted for Stonewall found that 82% of teachers found Section 28 confusing and 44% said they had difficulty addressing the needs of young LGBs because of it.

The message that gets through is that it is dangerous, even unlawful, to discuss lesbian and gay issues in schools (even though the law itself only relates to local authorities, which no longer control schools). This means that ignorance and homophobic bullying frequently go unchallenged, and young LGBs in schools do not get the support they deserve.

Section 28 has been repealed in Scotland, and is in the process of being repealed in England and Wales.

• The above information is an extract from Peer Support Project's web site which can be found at www.peer-support.org.uk Alternatively see page 41 for their address details.

© Peer Support Project

Now let's have real equality for lesbians and gay men

A mere two and a half years after MPs voted to equalise the age of consent for homosexual men at 16, Tony Blair has used the Parliament Act to overcome the House of Lords to put the measure on the statute book. This modest Bill to remove one element of discrimination has provoked a furious reaction – which speaks volumes for the sexual obsessions of its opponents.

However, Mr Blair should learn from his recent experience of confronting the demons of Eurosceptic prejudice and have the courage to take decisions that may seem unpopular but are right.

It is shocking, for example, that lesbians and gay men should have no legal protection against being sacked for being gay. Anti-gay prejudice may be rife, but Mr Blair should trust to the greater strength of the belief in fair play. That will eventually overcome the prejudice, but speeding up that process demands leadership.

This requires a simple law against unfair discrimination on grounds of sexual orientation. The 1950 European Convention on Human Rights offers only ambiguous protection to homosexuals. A clearer law would give gay partners pension rights, tenancy rights and rights to inheritance. But the Government resists this, because legal recognition of gay partnerships would be condemned by reactionaries as 'gay marriage'. This is not a shadow which should make ministers jump. Many homosexuals would like the public affirmation of marriage; why should they not have it?

The emotive issue is that of child-rearing, but it has to be recognised that the only good argument against gay couples raising children is the pressure on the children of popular prejudice. But many children face prejudice, and gay couples must by definition be unusually determined and committed parents. Equally, though, more needs to be done in schools to ensure that homosexuality is not used as a term of abuse and as an excuse for bullying, as the tragic case of Damilola Taylor demonstrated so painfully.

Mr Blair should take heart from doing the right thing yesterday, and press on with securing full equality for homosexual men and women.

© 2001 The Independent Newspaper (UK) Ltd

Transsexuals seek marriage rights

By Robert Verkaik, Legal Affairs Correspondent

The government could be forced to grant marriage rights to Britain's 5,000 transsexuals if a former nurse wins a legal battle to have her 'husband' benefit from her NHS pension.

Yesterday three Court of Appeal judges were told the Health Secretary's decision not to recognise the nurse's marriage to her transsexual husband, by refusing his right to her pension when she dies, breached their human rights and was discriminatory.

Under British law, transsexuals cannot alter their birth certificates and so cannot legally marry a person of the same birth sex. But during the hearing Lord Justice Aldous acknowledged that 'in reality' the nurse's husband 'is a man'. The court ordered anonymity for the nurse and her partner, who went through an adapted Church of England marriage ceremony.

> *Under British law, transsexuals cannot alter their birth certificates and so cannot legally marry a person of the same birth sex*

Laura Cox QC, representing the nurse, told Lord Justices Aldous, Brooke and Sedley that the case had been referred to them by the Employment Appeal Tribunal because of the 'fundamental human rights' elements. She said her client, a nurse and care manager for 20 years, was being supported by the pressure group Justice, and the Equal Opportunities Commission.

The employment tribunal had ruled there was no discrimination because under the pension rules the pair had to be married to benefit from her pension if he were to become a widower.

Ms Cox said: 'She complains that the benefits payable under the NHS pension scheme are being denied to her partner, a female to male transsexual, and this is discrimination on the grounds of sex.'

He had gone through a 'lengthy and painful process of treatment and operations' to be able to live in his true gender identity. 'He lives as a man, presents as a man and to all intents and purposes the couple present to the world as man and wife.' The Court of Appeal referred the case to the European Court of Justice. © 2001 The Independent Newspaper (UK) Ltd

ADDITIONAL RESOURCES

You might like to contact the following organisations for further information. Due to the increasing cost of postage, many organisations cannot respond to enquiries unless they receive a stamped, addressed envelope.

AVERT
4 Brighton Road
Horsham
West Sussex, RH13 5BA
Tel: 01403 210202
Fax: 01403 211001
E-mail: avert@dial.pipex.com
Web site: Web site: www.avert.org
AVERT is a leading UK AIDS Education and Medical Research charity. They are responsible for a wide range of education and medical research work. Publish a wide range of educational material on the issues of homosexuality. Ask for their Resources Catalogue.

Campaign For Homosexual Equality (CHE)
PO Box 342
London, WC1X 0DU
Tel: 07702 326151
The Campaign For Homosexual Equality (CHE) works to bring lesbians and gay men the same rights in society as heterosexual people take for granted.

Gay and Lesbian Humanist Association (GALHA)
GALHA National Office
34 Spring Lane
Kenilworth
Warwickshire, CV8 2HB
Tel: 01926 858450
E-mail: info@galha.org
Web site: www.galha.org/galha.htm
GALHA provides a voice for the many non-religious in the lesbian and gay community in the United Kingdom and elsewhere and promotes a rational humanist approach to homosexuality and to lesbian, gay and bisexual rights as human rights.

Gayteens
77c Aslett Street
London, SW18 2BE
E-mail: admin@gayteens.org
Web site: www.gayteens.org
The support and information site – for young people and their families and for those unsure of their sexuality.

Healthy Gay Scotland
18/19 Claremont Crescent
Edinburgh, EH4 7QD
Tel: 0131 556 3882
Fax: 0131 556 0279
E-mail: info@hgscotland.org.uk
Web site: www.hgscotland.org.uk
Healthy Gay Scotland devises and delivers a national programme of work which aims at preventing the spread of HIV among gay and bisexual men. Healthy Gay Scotland is funded by the Scottish Executive and is jointly managed by the Health Education Board for Scotland (HEBS) and the Scottish Voluntary HIV and AIDS Forum (SVHAF) with the National AIDS Trust as contract holder and a valuable source of information and advice.

Lesbian and Gay Employment Rights – LAGER
Unit 1G
Leroy House
436 Essex Road
London, N1 3QP
Tel: 020 7704 2205
Fax: 020 7704 6067
Web site: www.lager.dircon.co.uk
Works towards challenging all forms of discrimination faced by lesbians and gay men in the workplace including HIV/AIDS issues. Produces publications.

Lesbian & Gay Christian Movement (LGCM)
Oxford House
Derbyshire Street
London, E2 6HG
Tel/Fax: 020 7739 1249
E-mail: igcm@aol.com
Web site: www.lgcm.org.uk
One aim of the Lesbian & Gay Christian Movement is encourage fellowship, friendship, and support among individual lesbian and gay Christians through prayer, study and action. They run a counselling helpline on 020 7739 8134 on Wednesdays and Sundays from 7.00 pm-9.30pm.

Peer Support Project
PO Box 153
Manchester, M60 1LP
Tel: 0161 274 4664
Fax: 0161 274 4664
E-mail: office@peer-support.org.uk
Web site: www.peer-support.org.uk
The Peer Support Project provides peer support services for young (15-25) lesbians, gays and bisexuals in Greater Manchester.

Press for Change
BM Network
London, WC1N 3XX
Tel: 07836 344334
E-mail: editor@pfc.org.uk
Web site: www.pfc.org.uk
Press for Change is a political lobbying and educational organisation, which campaigns to achieve equal civil rights and liberties for all transgender people in the United Kingdom, through legislation and social change.

Stonewall Lobby Group Ltd
46 Grosvenor Gardens
London, SW1W 0EB
Tel: 020 7881 9440
Fax: 020 7222 0525
Web site: www.stonewall.org.uk
Works to achieve fully equal legal rights for lesbians and gay men in the UK, by providing information and support for legislators. Produces publications.

The Maranatha Community
102 Irlam Road
Flixton
Manchester, M41 6JT
Tel: 0161 748 4858
Fax: 0161 747 7379
Web site: www.maranathacommunity.org.uk
The Maranatha Community is a Christian movement which involves members of many different strands within the Christian faith. Their central aim is to become more effective Christians in life, work and worship.

INDEX

adoption, and gay couples 38
age of consent for gay sex 17, 19, 29-30, 39, 40
AIDS (Acquired Immune Deficiency Syndrome)
    and homosexuality 12, 17, 24

bisexuality 8, 9
boys and young men, prejudice towards gay people by 17
bullying, homophobic 18, 31, 40

Catholic Church
    and homosexuality 15
celibacy, and the Catholic Church 15
children
    dismissal of lesbian or gay employees having access to 34
    of gay couples 37, 40
    sexual pressures on 24-5
Christianity
    and homosexuality 5, 8, 12, 21, 24-6
        'curing' 5, 8, 20, 26
        early Christians 21
constructive dismissal, and lesbian and gay employees
    33-4
crime, compensation for criminal injuries and deaths 37

death, compensation for criminal injuries and deaths 37

employment, gay rights in the workplace 32-5
equal opportunities, in the workplace, and lesbian and
gay employees 35

families
    and gay couples 36-7
    and homophobia 18, 19

gay, use of the term 1, 2
gay couples
    children of 37, 40
    compensation for deaths as a result of crime 37
    rights of 30, 36-7
gay men
    and criminal convictions for sexual offences 34
    feeling about sexuality 7, 25, 29
    numbers of 25
    and promiscuity 15, 25
    public attitudes to 16
    and sex discrimination in the workplace 34
    see also homosexuality
genes, and homosexuality 7, 25, 26
Government policies
    on gays 17, 19
    on sex education 11

harassment, in the workplace, and lesbian and gay
    employees 35
heterosexuality
    assumptions of 3
    defining 2
    and gay lifestyles 6
    and homophobia 19-20

stereotypes of 3
homophobia 17-20
    and politics 18-19
    and religion 18
    and young people 17-18
homosexuality
    and AIDS 12, 17, 24
    and the Catholic Church 15
    and Christianity 5, 8, 12, 21, 24-6
    and 'coming out' 3, 9-10
    'curing' 5, 8, 20, 26
    defining 2-3, 24
    feelings developing in adulthood 7
    and the gay subculture 24
    and genetics 7, 25, 26
    and homophobia 17-20
    legal aspects of 5, 29-40
        age of consent 17, 19, 29-30, 39, 40
        employment protection 32-5
        and judges 36-7
        rights of gay couples 30, 36-7
        Section 28 of the Local Government Act 4, 18, 19,
          30, 31, 39
    and lifestyle 3, 6
    and marriage 3, 5, 36-7
        gay marriages 15, 19, 30, 38
    nature of 3-4
    negative images of 13
    objections to 12-13
    positive images of 13-14
    and prejudice 3-4, 14, 16, 17-18
    psycho-social explanations of 8, 18, 20, 25-6
    and sex education 10-12, 13-14, 18
    statistics on 36
    stereotypes of 3
    terminology 1, 2
    and young people 5, 7, 8, 10-12, 13-14, 19
        prejudice among 17-18
Human Rights Act, and homosexual marriages 38

judges
    and gay marriages 38
    guidelines for on the treatment of homosexuals
        36-7

lesbians
    public attitudes to 16
    and sex discrimination in the workplace 35
    use of the term 'lesbian' 1
    see also homosexuality
lifestyle, and sexuality 3, 6

marriage
    and homosexuality 3, 5
        gay marriages 15, 19, 30, 38
        guidelines for judges 36-7
    and sex education 10

social pressures against 25
and trans people 28, 40

National Curriculum, and sex education 10-11
Northern Ireland, age of consent 29

parents, of gay people, and 'coming out' 9, 10
prejudice, and homosexuality 3-4, 14, 16, 17-18
public attitudes
    to lesbians and gay men 16
    to Section 28 of the Local Government Act 4

Rastafarians 36
religious views
    on homosexuality 5, 8, 12, 18, 24-6
       and job discrimination 32-3

schools
    homophobic bullying in 18, 31
    and Section 28 of the Local Government Act 4, 18,
       19, 30, 31, 39
sex discrimination, in the workplace, and lesbians and
    gay men 34, 35
sex education
    Government policies on 11
    and homosexuality 10-12, 13-14, 18
sex offenders
    and abuse of trust 39
    dismissal from employment 34
    and gross indecency 39

sexual behaviour, and sexual feelings 2-3
social class, and attitudes towards homosexuality 17
suicide, and gay people 19

teachers, and sex education 14, 18
trans people 27-8
    and marriage 40

unfair dismissal, and lesbian and gay employees 33, 40

violence, attacks on gay people 14, 17, 19

workplace discrimination
    lesbian and gay employees 32-5
       civil remedies for 35
       constructive dismissal 33-4
       criminal convictions for sexual offences 34
       and equal opportunities policies 35
       harassment at work 35
       harassment as a criminal offence 35
       risk to children or young people 34
       unfair dismissal 33, 40

young people
    dismissal of lesbian or gay employees having access to 34
    and homosexuality 5, 7, 8
       images of 13-14, 19
       prejudice among 17-18
       and sex education 10-12, 13-14
       and suicide 19

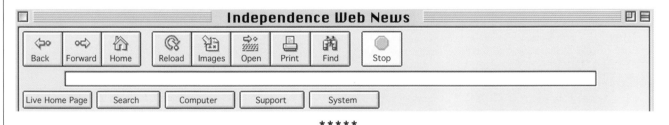

★★★★★

The Internet has been likened to shopping in a supermarket without aisles. The press of a button on a web browser can bring up thousands of sites but working your way through them to find what you want can involve long and frustrating on-line searches.

And unfortunately many sites contain inaccurate, misleading or heavily biased information. Our researchers have therefore undertaken an extensive analysis to bring you a selection of quality web site addresses.

AVERT
www.avert.org
This site focuses mainly on information on HIV education and prevention but there is also a lot of information on homosexuality. This information includes advice and statistics. Click on the <u>Homosexuality</u> link to view a list of topics covered including, Am I gay?, Defining homosexuality, Public attitudes to gay men and The age of (sexual) consent. There is also information for young people on the issue of homosexuality.

Gayteens
www.gayteens.org
The support and information site – for young people and their families and for those unsure of their sexuality. This is a brilliant site with stacks of information. Fun pages for teenagers.

Lesbian Information Service (LIS)
www.lesbinform.fsnet.co.uk
This is an extensive web site with information on many topics affecting lesbians.

Gay to Z
www.gaytoz.com
Great web site with loads of information and links. There are, however, adult material contacts here.

Stonewall Lobby Group Ltd
www.stonewall.org.uk
A brilliant web site packed with information. Firstly you need to highlight what kind of viewer you are, the choices include <u>Lesbian or gay visitor</u>, <u>Young person</u> and <u>Parent or teacher</u>. Then you can visit various sections of the web site including love, work, school, partnership to view articles on various topics within that section.

ACKNOWLEDGEMENTS

The publisher is grateful for permission to reproduce the following material.

While every care has been taken to trace and acknowledge copyright, the publisher tenders its apology for any accidental infringement or where copyright has proved untraceable. The publisher would be pleased to come to a suitable arrangement in any such case with the rightful owner.

Chapter One: Addressing Sexuality

Homosexual or gay?, © AVERT, *Sexual feelings and behaviour*, © AVERT, *Homosexuality is . . .* , © Campaign for Homosexual Equality (CHE), *Section 28*, © Stonewall, *Christianity and homosexuality*, © Lesbian & Gay Christian Movement (LGCM), *Straights and gays take to same lifestyle*, © Guardian Newspapers Limited 2001, *Questions*, © AVERT, *Coming out*, © Healthy Gay Scotland, *Sex education*, © Stonewall, *Calling for honesty in education*, © Campaign for Homosexual Equality (CHE), *Homosexuality*, © Scottish Catholic Media Office, *Prejudice and discrimination*, © MORI, *Attitudes to lesbians and gay men*, © Citizenshipship 21/ Stonewall, *Prejudice against gay men*, © AVERT, *Background to homophobia*, © Gay Teens, *Fury over gay study*, © The Daily Mail, May 2001, *Homosexuality and the church*, © Lesbian & Gay Christian Movement (LGCM), *Lesbians, gay men, bisexuals and mental health*, © MIND, *Identity and sexuality*, © The Maranatha Community, *What is the gay gene?*, © Stonewall, *Press for Change*, © Press for Change.

Chapter Two: The Legal Aspects

Age of consent, © Stonewall, *Age of consent*, © Stonewall, *New battle for gay couples' rights*, © Guardian Newspapers Limited 2001, *Section 28*, © Stonewall, *Gay job protection soon*, © 2000 The Gay and Lesbian Humanist Association (GALHA), *Discrimination against lesbian and gay employees*, © 2001 Lesbian and Gay Employment Rights (LAGER), *Be biased in favour of gays judges are told*, © The Daily Mail, December 2000, *Gay partners will get crime payouts*, © The Daily Mail, February 2001, *Gay marriages*, © The Daily Mail, October 2000, *Laws relating to young LGBs*, © Peer Project Support, *Now let's have real equality for lesbians and gay men*, © 2001 The Independent Newspaper (UK) Ltd, *Transsexuals seek marriage rights*, © 2001 The Independent Newspaper (UK) Ltd.

Photographs and illustrations:

Pages 1, 6, 9, 14, 38: Pumpkin House, pages 8, 11, 13, 15, 21, 27, 32, 34, 39: Simon Kneebone.

Craig Donnellan
Cambridge
September, 2001